The First Overland Mail

THE FIRST

OVERLAND MAIL

★

by ROBERT E. PINKERTON

Illustrated by PAUL LANTZ

Landmark BOOKS

RANDOM HOUSE · NEW YORK

Copyright 1953 by Robert E. Pinkerton

All rights reserved under International and
Pan-American Copyright Conventions

Published in New York by Random House, Inc.
and simultaneously in Toronto, Canada by
Random House of Canada Ltd.

Library of Congress Catalog Card Number: 53–6259

Manufactured in the U. S. A.

To the men who drove the stagecoaches

1

THE STAGECOACH WAS SUPREME IN 1801. IT carried the United States mail, and its passengers were important people bound on business or government affairs. Others walked or rode horses, and few went more than a few miles from home. Freight moved slowly behind ox teams.

The glamor and romance of travel and far places centered in the stagecoach, in its speed and the dash of its horses, in the clatter of its passing. Men in fields waved their hats. Children in villages shouted, "Here she comes!" Dogs in towns raced beside the spinning wheels. Men gathered at stations where teams were changed. Women looked from their weaving to the grandfather's clock and said, "Henry Buckley's on time, as usual."

It was the horse in 1801, and nothing except the horse if you were in a hurry, but it was the drivers that people watched and admired. Most were quiet men, aware of their responsibility and careful of their horses and keeping schedule. Others added the quality of an actor. They'd save their teams for a final burst of speed, take the stage into town on the gallop and come to a dramatic stop. Departures were more theatrical with fresh teams racing madly.

In November of that same year, 1801, John Butterfield was born on his father's farm west of Albany, New York, and if he hadn't lived on a stage route he might have become a farmer as did

most of his acquaintances. Before he could walk, his mother would carry him to the road when the stage was due. As the horses dashed past, the child grew more and more excited.

"I often wondered if I marked him, doing that," she once said. "He got so worked up over it."

After John Butterfield could use his legs, he kept his own time schedule, as young children and animals do so accurately. Only in the worst weather did he fail to stand beside the road when the stage went by. Stage drivers began to notice him. He'd be there, rain or snow or freezing weather, waving his arms. When John was five,

Henry Buckley blew his long coaching horn a half mile from the Butterfield farm. As this was sounded only on approach to stage stations, the boy listened in ecstasy. He felt suddenly that he was part of stagecoaching. Next day he led his mother to hear the entrancing music.

"Looks grand, don't it?" she said, awed by the special salute to her son and by the driver's lifted hat.

"It goes so fast," the boy said.

Years later, Mrs. Butterfield told of this. "I knew right then nothing else would ever satisfy him," said she. "John was going to be a stage-coach driver."

John talked to his father of his excitement.

"What's a stagecoach without horses?" Daniel Butterfield asked. "Like a preacher who's lost his tongue. Or a skillet without a fire. If it's stage-coachin' you want, learn what makes 'em go. It's

4

a four-legged critter called a horse. Quit lookin'
at the coaches and look at what keeps 'em run-
nin'."

Next day he went with his son when the horn
sounded.

"Don't look at the people in the wagon," he
said. "Or at Henry Buckley. Where'd he be
without horses? Watch their footwork—the off
leader's spavined. Watch how they're built. Near
wheel horse is short coupled, nice mare. Watch
their ears. That tells if an animal's got git-up-
and-go. It's the horses that draws the stages."

After that John studied their conformation and
leg action, how they carried their heads. His
father talked to him of draft breeds, of lighter
and faster strains, and explained the care of horses,
how to look for diseases or injuries, how to judge
the temperament of an animal and how to handle
it. When John was ten years old, he knew a great

deal about horses. Also at ten he was a hard working farm boy, being spared only to go to the country school. He arrived breathless from morning chores and hurried home for the evening work and care of horses.

More and more his father was aware he had a future stagecoach driver as a son, and that was all right. It meant a step up from the drudgery of farm work. Nor did John, when he was a boy, think past driving a coach. This was the most exciting thing in his world, and he wanted a part in it.

His world was not large, and much of it was little known. In 1801, when he was born, the United States extended only to the Mississippi River. Beyond the Appalachian Mountains was a vast territory into which few had penetrated. More than two-thirds of our present nation was in the hands of European states, and Americans knew nothing of it. The new Republic clung to the Atlantic seaboard, but even Florida and the Gulf of Mexico coast belonged to Spain. In the west was a vast territory owned by France, and beyond that was another great expanse in Spanish domain that extended to the Pacific.

When John Butterfield was two years old, his country negotiated the Louisiana Purchase at a cost of $11,250,000. Napoleon Bonaparte evidently needed money or considered the land of little value. It extended from the Gulf of Mexico to the present Canadian border and included what we now know as Arkansas, Missouri, Nebraska, Iowa, North and South Dakota; most of Louisiana, Oklahoma, and Kansas; and even much of Minnesota, Montana, Wyoming, and Colorado. No nation ever acquired so vast and rich a land for so little —four cents an acre.

Not many Americans knew what this meant.

7

They were busy making a living along the Atlantic seaboard. Only a few had dared cross the mountains into Western Pennsylvania and Kentucky. Most men, thinking of their farms and small businesses, saw no need for expansion.

The mechanical age dawned before John Butterfield was six years old, when Robert Fulton made the first steamboat voyage, from New York to Albany, 150 miles, in thirty-two hours. The War of 1812 occupied the country's attention, and the small republic failed to look at its new rich lands in the west. In 1817 work was begun on the Erie Canal.

The nation grew slowly. In 1820 it had less than ten million people. In that year John Butterfield decided to leave the farm for stagecoaching. He got a job in Albany with the Parker Line which hired him to drum up business for its stages. Before he was twenty he was handling the reins,

8

snapping the whip, dashing into and out of towns as Henry Buckley had done, but he was not satisfied.

Working for someone else wasn't enough. He wanted to own the horses he drove and the coaches. To save money he lived in the stable, his bed on the hay. When he had enough, he bought a horse and buggy and began his own livery business while still a stage driver.

This was common in 1821—a young fellow working long hours and pinching every penny. In no other way could he get ahead. Also it was common for a young man to marry early to have a helpmate. So before he was old enough to vote, John Butterfield had a wife, Malinda Baker. They opened a boarding house and thereby earned more money. John drove stages less and less. He was advanced by the Parker Line until he became manager.

The world of transportation lay before him. All the money he and his wife could save was put into horses and stagecoaches. He started branch lines north and south from the Albany-Buffalo route. Twenty years after he left his father's farm, he controlled nearly all stage lines west of Albany.

Before this achievement a new factor entered the American scene. In 1830 the Baltimore and Ohio Railroad Company operated a passenger train. The line was fourteen miles long and, while its cars ran on wooden rails plated with iron, the motive power was still the horse. A year later a railroad train drawn by a steam engine covered the fifteen-mile route from Albany to Schenectady in New York.

This was something different. It was in the center of John Butterfield's stagecoach domain. With shriek and grunt and thick wood smoke,

The first trains were a threat to the stagecoach lines

the iron horse was a threat to his empire. Stage-coaches could not compete with a roaring train, but John Butterfield was not disturbed. Fifteen miles was nothing compared with his long routes, and what if this newfangled contraption did stretch its clanging length to Buffalo? The side routes remained, leading north to Lake Ontario and south into Pennsylvania. Horses would still draw stagecoaches.

John Butterfield was not a stubborn fool for all his love of horse and coach. If he couldn't lick steam power, he could join it. He branched from stages to steamships on the Great Lakes, to a steam railroad in Utica and an early horse-drawn street-car. In 1845 he was wealthy, a leading citizen in Utica. Later he became mayor.

With the railroad expanding, a new business opened. Henry Wells and William G. Fargo each organized an express company to handle light goods more swiftly. Until then small parcels had moved by ox team and canal boat. In 1849 John Butterfield formed his own express company. The three concerns were in direct competition, and Butterfield proposed a combination. Wells and Fargo agreed and the American Express Company, still in existence, was the result.

Railroads continued to spread, and John Butterfield's stage lines to dwindle. He knew that in time stagecoaches would be doomed everywhere, and he looked for a new pioneering enterprise. With Henry Wells and others he formed the New York, Albany and Buffalo Telegraph Company, one of the first.

John Butterfield owned much real estate in Utica, had built a fine residence, a hotel and a business block. He had a family of four sons and three daughters, and those who wished went to college. The farm boy who watched the stages dash past had come a long way, but for all his success he still longed for the clatter of hoofs and rattle of wheels, for the music of a coaching horn. The puffing of locomotives seemed to be burying such sounds forever.

2

SEVERAL THINGS BEGAN TO HAPPEN BEFORE AND after John Butterfield formed the American Express Company in 1849. He did not see that some were signs of future trends. Least of all did he suspect that the horse-drawn stage, which he considered dying, was about to enter its greatest and most glamorous phase. Nor did John Butterfield foresee that he would be the architect of this final glory of the coach and four, that his horses and mules would dash—and really dash—from the Mississippi River to the Pacific Ocean.

The first significant event was the War with Mexico. When peace came in 1848, the United States had expanded to its present limits, except for the Gadsden Purchase made five years later. The nation extended from the Atlantic across the continent and from Canada to Mexico.

Trouble was, the nation didn't understand what this could and did mean. Its citizens had reached the Mississippi. Beyond was the "Great American Desert," a term long to remain in the minds of a generation of school children though it included Oklahoma, Kansas, Nebraska, eastern Colorado, Wyoming and the Dakotas. People knew little or nothing about the area beyond the Mississippi yet it comprises two-thirds of the country today.

The Hudson's Bay Company, seeking only fur, had explored Idaho, Montana, Washington, Oregon, Utah, Nevada and all California but its leaders kept their mouths shut. In 1806 Lewis and Clark returned from their expedition to the Pacific Northwest. In 1821 American ox-hauled wagons reached Santa Fe, ancient Mexican town. First Americans to go from Santa Fe to California were James Ohio Pattie and his father. "Mountain men" pressed into the West from Canada to Mexico. Adventurers all, they were the sort who had to see "what was beyond the next hill."

Fur traders, trappers, men "just going to have a look"—most were illiterate, those who could write left slim records, and many never returned. For years they probed the West with few reports of where they had gone and what they had seen. Only the Mormons in Utah and settlers who had made the long ox-train journey to Oregon were known. Those east of the Mississippi had slight interest in the rest of the nation.

Then, on the far side of this great land, gold

exploded in California—the most sensational event in America's history so far. Men went west any way they could—around The Horn in sailing ships, across the Isthmus of Panama, by ox train

People went wild when gold was discovered in California

and prairie schooner over the great plains and two mountain ranges. Some land routes were known, as the well-worn Oregon trail and the path of the Mormons to Salt Lake City. In the far southwest the Army had blazed, and only blazed, roads in 1846.

Yet this vast country was almost entirely unmapped and wholly unknown to those who thought only of getting to California before all the gold was mined. Men with no knowledge of the West developed all sorts of theories and acted on them. The result was that impossible trails were marked by the white skeletons of horses, oxen and men.

Those who had lived along the Atlantic coast could not comprehend high mountains, or deserts in which no water was to be found and where the temperature rose to 125 degrees in the shade. They could not imagine the deep snows of the

18

Trails were marked by the skeletons of men and beasts

Rocky Mountains and especially those of the Sierra Nevada. There the annual fall of snow may be twenty to thirty feet, and the record is more than seventy feet.

They were children, those gold seekers, in an undreamed-of land. Many died, many turned back. Others, with that strange gold-driven courage, thirsted through the heat of the deserts, wallowed through the snows of the mountains and flowed into California by the thousand. When they had settled, they demanded mail from home. Mormons, already established in Utah, had asked for this service, and in 1850 the Post Office Department awarded a contract to carry mail between the Missouri River and Salt Lake City. The next year a contract was made to continue the route to Placerville, first known as Hangtown, in California.

This was the beginning of a series of stagecoach attempts, many of which failed. Men made bids, got contracts, sold them to others. It was too tough. Winter snows would not let the coaches through. Some contracts provided for mail delivery by snowshoes. For a time a Norwegian, known as "Snowshoe Thompson," was chief letter carrier across the Sierra Nevada. Many

The Civil War threatened like a storm on the horizon

tribes of Indians provided serious trouble from eastern Nebraska through Nevada, killing drivers and passengers, as they did until the railroad was completed nearly twenty years later.

Indians and snow were lesser difficulties. Political trickery, sectional rivalries solid in the South but split in the North, efforts of men to make easy money, and the long maneuvering before the War Between the States—these delayed a successful stage route across the continent for years. Arguments in Congress and out were violent. It was astonishing how many senators and editors, men who had never crossed the Allegheny Mountains, became authorities on what the West was like, how easy it was to traverse, or how impossible.

John Butterfield, the man with stagecoaches in his blood and the sound of a stage horn always in his ears, kept close track of what went on in Washington and across the Mississippi. He understood the political battles and sectional rivalries, knew what they were worth, but what drew him was the challenge in the physical problem of carrying mail and passengers so far. He read War Department reports of early expeditions, post office reports on contracts and how lines had failed, and the few books written by travelers.

He learned of earlier trading and military roads in the Southwest, details of the Oregon trail, and to get facts he could trust he sent one of his stage drivers from the Mohawk Valley to San Francisco and back on the central or Salt Lake City route. Months passed before the man returned, and what he had to tell of difficulties and careless operation was dismaying.

"John, you'd die of a stroke the first day out there," the driver said. "One look at how they run stages would do it. Those birds never heard what you told us every day of the year."

"What's that?" Butterfield asked with a growl.

" 'Remember, boys! Nothing on God's earth must stop the United States mail.' I can hear you in my sleep."

Butterfield grunted. He couldn't look back on those days. He was looking ahead.

"The mail's stopped plenty out there," the

23

driver said. "If it ain't a lead horse steppin' in a prairie dog hole, or the handlers not having a fresh team ready, or the driver being drunk, or the horses dying o' thirst, it's the Indians. I saw enough of 'em, and heard more. Me—I'd rather hire out to the devil and run a coach through purgatory."

Like everything else about this fabulous country, the Mohawk Valley driver's report only added to the challenge. John Butterfield gathered all information available, and none of it was encouraging. The route would be 2,000 to 2,500 miles, distances unknown in the East. In New York, oats and hay were cheap and obtainable anywhere. Water ran in countless brooks. Farms lined the post roads and taverns provided meals and overnight lodgings.

Beyond the Mississippi there were no towns, no farms, no taverns, no sources of horse feed and, in long stretches, no water. Also thousands of Indians were waiting to attack stages, run off stock and kill passengers and drivers.

A man would be crazy to dare such an enterprise, but John Butterfield was fascinated by the challenge and kept digging for more information and making plans. Hard as he had worked in the Mohawk Valley, his routes there were easy compared with hauling mail and passengers to the Pacific.

Meanwhile politicians and sectional interests fought. The North was divided, the South solid, and the Postmaster General was from Tennessee. In June, 1857, he awarded a contract to carry mail and passengers from San Antonio in Texas to San Diego in California, 1,475 miles, all close to the Mexican border. James E. Birch, a young New Englander who ran stages in California, got the job, agreeing to make two journeys a month each way. He was given thirty days for each trip.

After he started his organization, he embarked from San Francisco for New York and drowned when the ship sank.

San Diego was 600 miles from the gold fields, and Californians protested. Finally Congress passed an act providing for a through route from the Mississippi to San Francisco. This is what John Butterfield had been waiting for. He wished to run his own stages all the way and would take nothing else. With several others he organized the Overland Mail Company with capital of $2,000,000—a large sum in those days.

Still the battle went on, with politicians, editors and sectional interests shouting objections. Again the South won. The Postmaster General selected a route so far south it even dipped into Mexico. On September 16, 1857, he signed an agreement with the Overland Mail Company. In effect, John Butterfield was the Overland Mail.

3

STILL THE BATTLE WENT ON IN CONGRESS AND the newspapers. The six bidders who failed to get the contract called the Overland Mail Company a stock-jobbing enterprise. Editors said the route chosen was impossible. Advocates of northern routes blasted the project. Though the East took little interest in the matter, the common belief was that the Overland Mail never intended to run stages and, after selling shares, would drop out. Many people in the West said terms of the contract made it impossible to operate, that the mail would never go through.

John Butterfield gave no heed to all that was said and printed. No task in American transportation has been so great as that he faced. He had no time for bickerings. He had a stagecoach job, and he faced it with exultation, and also fear. More than once he doubted he could fulfill the contract.

That contract's terms were enough to frighten any man. It provided annual payment of $600,-000 for a semi-weekly service, in addition to fares for passengers carried. But——

The route was 2,800 miles long and each trip must be made in twenty-five days! Further, the overland mail must be operating in one year!

That meant 112 miles each day, in any weather, despite any obstacles. In New York State, with good roads and frequent changes of horses, ten miles an hour was possible in level country by day. But in the West there were no roads as Easterners knew them. In half the route not a shovel or pick had been used. The Mohawk Valley roads were level. This course led across high plateaus and two high mountain ranges.

In the East, post roads passed through towns and villages. But on John Butterfield's line, after Fort Smith in Arkansas, there were only two small towns before Los Angeles was reached—El Paso and Tucson. In one stretch of more than 900 miles *no white man lived*.

And Indians! First were the Comanches in West Texas. They had kept whites out of that country since they first appeared. Where the Comanches left off, the Apaches took over. They ruled for about 600 miles, to the Colorado River. Beyond were hostile tribes in Mexico. These Indians hated white men and often with good reason.

How about feed for horses? Mexicans along

the Rio Grande above El Paso raised crops. A few settlers in eastern Oklahoma did likewise. Elsewhere, until California was reached, were no hay or oats. And water! None in one stretch of seventy-five miles. Another of forty in the Arizona desert! Horses couldn't travel that far without it in intense heat.

And always! Each trip of 2,800 miles in twenty-five days.

It couldn't be done. No one who had been in that part of the West believed it possible. But the West was not stagecoach country. It had no stagecoach man like John Butterfield of New York State. He was determined to prove it could be done. Before he died, he wanted to see the stagecoach again supreme.

He had been ready long before the contract was signed. He had sent engineers to California to survey the route from that end. He had engineers ready to start from St. Louis. He had sent scouts to Ohio and Kentucky to pick up the best stage drivers, and he had the core of his own experienced men in New York State. The best of these had been selected as superintendents of the nine divisions into which the 2,800-mile route was separated.

The push-button age had not arrived a century ago, but John Butterfield had something like it. The moment the Postmaster General signed the contract, orders went out. All had been arranged for equipment needed, for mobilization of men, for distribution of supplies, for building stations, for purchase of arms for defense against Indians, for a thousand things that must be provided for so huge an enterprise. Each detail had been worked out in advance, or so John Butterfield hoped. He knew what was needed in the Mohawk Valley. The West—he had never seen it.

Nothing in all the history of stagecoaching has approached in magnitude the preparations necessary for the Overland Mail. To maintain schedule, sixteen coaches, eight in each direction, must be on the road at all times. They must travel night and day for twenty-five days, must never stop except for team changes. Teams would have four, five or six horses, depending on the nature of the roads and country. To do this,

John Butterfield bought 2,000 horses.

He placed an order for 250 stagecoaches.

He ordered scores of large freight wagons.

He bought many hundred sets of harness.

He bought shovels and picks in lots of a dozen gross.

He bought stage horns, halters, thousands of horseshoes, horseshoe nails, equipment for dozens of blacksmith shops, all the many articles needed in the care of coaches and horses. In that year of preparation he spent $1,000,000.

All that he bought was loaded on trains for St. Louis or was poured into ships to be taken to San Francisco and started from that end. Still John Butterfield had no assurance of success.

4

John butterfield was a big man with a thick square body and a square face. He looked as if nothing could beat him, and now when nearly fifty-seven years old he had not lost his aggressive vigor. But when he sat in his office at 84 Broadway in New York City after signing the contract to carry the mail to San Francisco, he often had moments of doubt and of fear.

He looked up from his desk and saw a cross-stitch motto on the wall. The wife of one of his drivers had made it, using the words he spoke so often when his stagecoaches ran from Albany to Buffalo.

"Remember, boys! Nothing on God's earth must stop the United States mail!"

He'd been saying this seventy-five years before the famous motto was carved on the New York post office: "Neither snow nor rain nor heat nor gloom of night stays these couriers from the swift completion of their appointed rounds."

John Butterfield looked away from the cross-stitched words in a walnut frame.

"Which means," he muttered, "that I've got to start it for 'em. And only three hundred and sixty-five days!"

He'd pressed the buttons. Everything was under way, but he still faced that great unknown —Oklahoma, Texas, New Mexico and Arizona, the great plains, the deserts, the mountains, the unbelievable distances, and always the Indians.

35

The door opened and a young man entered with a long roll of paper under an arm. He was John Butterfield, Jr., "Young John," and for him the older man had an extra affection. Young John was a stagecoach man too, had loved stage-coaches in his youth and had been a fine reinsman on the Butterfield lines in the Mohawk Valley. Like his father, he had the song of the stage horn in his ears.

"We could beat that train from Washington!" he said angrily. "Left yesterday and just got here. This map fellow's been through all the War Department, the Post Office Department and everything else the government has. Reports, maps, anything! I grabbed the map he made while it was still wet. Been studying it all the way. Nothing new."

John Butterfield unrolled it on his desk, his eyes seeking at once the white spaces from the

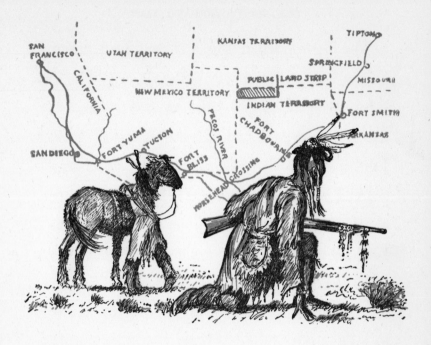

The route of the Overland Mail made almost a half circle

Mississippi River to the Pacific and finding the same old dotted lines across wide blanks.

"Here's the old Santa Fe Trail," young John said, pointing. "Doesn't help us any. Way north of where we have to go. This, across the Llano Estacado, is where Captain Pope went four years ago. Doesn't mean a road. He was hittin' out new, across nothing. Below him is General Marcy's trail in 1849. Same sort of thing."

"What's this one, heading southwest from Independence in Missouri?" the father asked.

"That's Connelly, in 1839. Haulin' trade goods down in Mexico, to Chihuahua. He used wagons, but he wasn't headin' for California. Probably no sign of him left."

"This?"

"One of those fool railroad surveys along the thirty-fifth parallel," young John said. "Postmaster General wouldn't have it. We've got to go here," and he swept a finger in a long arc.

John Butterfield smiled, took a fine steel chain from a pocket and went to a large map on the wall.

"Hold this end on St. Louis," he said. "I'll hold the other on San Francisco. There! A little more slack so we'll get into Mexico. That's right. And look at it. Almost half a circle."

"Twenty-eight hundred miles, and eight hundred shorter straight across. That way, through the middle, we could do it."

"Snow," said John Butterfield. "It would stop us twice, in the Rockies and the Sierra Nevada. And politics. The Postmaster General is a Southerner. Wants a line the South can control if war comes. The South needs that gold in California. They won't get it, but this is mail. The United States mail. The North's got to get mail through to California or California might join the South. That's our job."

Young John shrugged. He could send four horses galloping in front of a heavy stage, handle reins expertly, but politics and blank spaces on the map were beyond his comprehension. He swept a hand across them.

"Nothing!" he exclaimed. "Just nothing! Ten times as far as our line from Albany to Buffalo. Nobody's even tried to lick it. How you goin' to?"

"I've got to," John Butterfield said. "And you —aren't you a stagecoach man?"

He looked again at the map, studied it closely, following trails with a thick finger.

"Roads!" he snorted. "Because General Kearny went there or Colonel Cooke this way! Taking four hundred men and a few wagons across a country doesn't make a road. Kearny even dropped his wagons. Leach surveyed this trail, but that doesn't mean he built a road. He just passed through. So did the others. The Army's spent a lot of money west of El Paso claiming they were making a road, but most of it's off our route. Only one we can follow out there is the one the Jim Birch Line is starting, San Antonio to San

Diego, and we'll have only part of it. Probably nothing but wagon tracks."

He stood up and looked again at the cross-stitch motto.

"Son," he said, "we'll carry the mail across all that white paper. Somehow! Keep that idea in your head."

Soon afterward, John Butterfield moved his headquarters to St. Louis, and took Young John with him. There he found a town such as he had never seen. Several railroads had reached the Mississippi, but St. Louis was still the steamboat center of the nation. More than sixty companies operated river craft from St. Paul to New Orleans, up the Ohio to Pittsburgh and up the Missouri and several other tributaries.

At first there was interest in the Overland Mail project, but when no stagecoaches appeared and no mail was carried west, St. Louis forgot it. Steamboats were stopping every few hours, with their dramatic whistles and churning of paddle wheels, with many passengers and mounds of freight. Prairie schooners and their people, hungry for land, were being ferried across to swarm into Kansas and Nebraska. No one cared about stage-coaches.

John Butterfield scarcely noticed. He had a job, and he was still working in the dark. The engineers and road finders he had started from St. Louis and San Francisco were somewhere on those white spaces the maps showed, but no reports had come from them. Still he began to shovel men and equipment into the void of which he knew so little. Trains of huge freight wagons, with wide iron tires and carrying all the supplies that could be loaded on them, streamed into the southwest. They carried hay and oats, food for employees, tools for building stations, men to patch the worst places on the trail, candles for light, the scores of things needed for a project crossing a vast emptiness, for a project no one believed could succeed.

"If we can build a hundred stations in the next eleven months, we'll be doing well," John Butterfield said to his son. "And that means only one to every twenty-eight miles."

"Teams can't travel that far," Young John said. "You got to have more changes or you'll kill the horses."

"We need two hundred and fifty stations. We'll have 'em some day. Now a hundred's the best we can hope for."

John Butterfield kept the supplies moving into the southwest but still he had not heard from his engineers. He knew they were out there working hard, and yet couldn't tell him what they had

In some spots early settlers acted as station agents and

learned, whether the route was impossible for
fast service. Weeks would go by before he got
the first reports, and they weren't too good when
they came. Empty stretches, lack of water, no

ad fresh teams harnessed and ready for the stagecoaches

horse feed, rocky passes not wide enough to let
a coach through, hostile Indians—a stage route
through such a land, especially on a fast schedule,
was impossible.

45

Maps and reports kept John Butterfield up late at night. He studied them as a gem dealer might examine rough diamonds. His memory was remarkable and mile by mile he stowed away the information relayed to him. Later his engineers were astonished when he reeled off those miles, all 2,800 of them, never missing a detail and asking embarrassing questions as to why this detour from a straight line, why leave a used trail there.

He had one advantage only. The Pacific Railroad Company of Missouri, first to build tracks west of the Mississippi, had already reached Jefferson City and expected to have a line to Tipton, 160 miles west of St. Louis, when the stages were to start. From there to Fort Smith, on the Arkansas-Oklahoma border, was a military road built by the War Department. This promised to be an easy route but it passed through the western

Ozark Mountains and was, despite the Army's work, one of the roughest sections of the entire journey.

"If this is bad," John Butterfield growled, "what is the rest, with no roads, going to be like?"

He sent out more wagon trains with crews of men to work on the worst places of the road. He sent them on into Indian Territory, the present Oklahoma, where no work had been done, and on into West Texas, where much of the country was practically unknown, and in which no white men lived.

Before his men reached that area, John Butterfield selected early settlers to act as station agents, to care for horses and equipment, to have fresh teams harnessed and ready when the stage arrived. Such stopping places were known as "home stations," the owner working for the company.

47

Houses were seldom more than one or two-room log cabins. At meal stops the settler's wife cooked the food.

But beyond southeastern Oklahoma the company must build its own stations, southwest across Texas and all the way to the Colorado River and California. Even in the golden state, as far as Los Angeles, and in the dip into Mexico, buildings and corrals must be erected, provisioned and staffed. This in itself was a huge task. John Butterfield, remaining in St. Louis, worked long hours, kept every detail in his head, knew where each long freight train was, what it was doing.

At last he had final reports from engineers who had surveyed the entire route, but he was not satisfied.

"Every man on this job is an easterner," he said to Young John. "Except those in California. They were easterners too a few years ago and know

48

nothing of the southwest. I'm an easterner. Never saw this country. It's so different I'm not sure I understand it. You can't. We've got the best stage drivers in the world, but they know only good roads."

Young John had just returned from a trip to Fort Smith.

"If they call that a road, we'll be rolling coaches down mountainsides," he said. "And what the engineers tell me about a thousand miles beyond! One said he never wanted to see it again."

"That's it. Seems to scare them. It will scare our drivers when they get out there. What I want is a man who's used to it, who knows it, who's been through it time and again. The engineers saw it once and they've had enough. So you take the next boat to New Orleans. Take the ship to Indianola in Texas and the stage to San Antonio. Get me that man."

"We don't go anywhere near San Antonio," Young John said.

"No, but the Jim Birch Line is supposed to be running from San Antonio to San Diego. We take their route from El Paso until we cross the Colorado desert. Hang around their starting station. Listen to the drivers and conductors. Pick out the smartest you can find and bring him back."

Young John was gone a month. He returned to St. Louis in the spring of 1858. With him was a slender young fellow whom he introduced as Silas St. John. John Butterfield liked him at once, and more as they talked, especially when he learned St. John was also a New Yorker.

"Wonder that anyone's left at home," Butterfield said. "We all seem to be from there."

St. John was born in New York in 1835 and

before he was eighteen he started west from the Mississippi with an ox train, spending 167 days on the journey to California. After mining for a year he worked for two pioneer railroads in the Sacramento Valley until the fall of 1857, when he went to San Diego for the Jim Birch Line.

"Then you were in at the beginning," John Butterfield said.

"I rode the first mail going east, from Carrizo Creek to Yuma, last November the sixteenth," St. John said. "We made the hundred and ten miles in thirty-two hours."

"What! We've got to do better than that every twenty-four hours. Didn't they meet the contract terms?"

"No. Birch agreed to cover the fourteen hundred and seventy-five miles in thirty days with coach and four-horse teams. He wasn't ready and sent the first mail through on horseback. The next trip, with a coach, took thirty-eight days. He never beat that much."

"And we've got to do twice the distance in twenty-five days," John Butterfield said. "I knew this was tough, but not that tough."

5

JOHN BUTTERFIELD WAS WORRIED. IF JIM BIRCH, an experienced California stage man, couldn't make better time, how could he expect to? He sat up late, making estimates and figuring schedules, and always the answer was the same—112 miles daily in each of twenty-five successive days. One slip, a broken axle, an Indian attack, and he'd fail to meet the contract.

Jim Birch hadn't met the terms but John Butterfield suspected the Postmaster General, intent on a wholly southern route, was lenient. He wouldn't be lenient with the Overland Mail because he didn't like Butterfield. The Postmaster General had tried to make the eastern terminus at Memphis, or even Vicksburg, far south in Mississippi, and Butterfield had beaten him by suggesting a split ending, one at Memphis and the other at St. Louis. This meant he had to operate an additional 322 miles from Memphis to Fort Smith, 3,122 miles in all, and he felt sure that if he slipped up on one trip the Postmaster General would cancel the contract. After a million or more dollars had been spent!

In the next week John Butterfield talked several times with Silas St. John and liked him more. Young as he was, St. John had a good head, and he had experience. He'd been over a large part of the route in a stagecoach which no Butterfield man had done, had made three round trips as conductor between San Diego and San Antonio. He knew the road, the conditions, and his information was more valuable than the engineers had gathered.

"How many stations did Birch build?" Butterfield asked.

"None."

"What! No stations? How can they change horses and drivers? How do they store grain and supplies?"

"They don't," St. John said. "Each night they make camp after doing about forty miles. The horses graze and carry on next day."

"What do the passengers do?"

"Sleep on the ground. Cook their own meals over a campfire. Stand guard against Indian attacks."

John Butterfield was appalled. He jumped up and paced across his office.

"How they expect to get mail through that

way?" he shouted. "What the passengers going to think, being treated like that? No wonder they don't make time. You mean they just stop beside the road and camp?"

"Mostly," St. John said. "Passengers have to carry their own blankets. In a few camping places, always near water, of course, they have brush wickiups. Like the Apaches'. In one or two camps they've roofed them with adobe. Plastered mud, you know. They have stations in El Paso and Maricopa Wells where they can change teams and coaches, but they are far apart. You can hear the dry axles shrieking for miles. Indians always know when the stages are coming."

"What if they break an axle, or a coach turns over? Where's the mail then? Where's the passengers?"

"Oh, the driver would take the best horse and ride to the nearest station—San Antone, El Paso,

The stagecoach line had to go through the sandy desert

Yuma or San Diego. He'd get help in a week or two, if he got through."

John Butterfield stopped pacing and stood before St. John.

"Know what we're going to do?" he demanded. "We're going to run a stage line. We're going to run our stages night and day. For twenty-five days! Without stopping! We're going to have two hundred and fifty stations. We'll change horses every fifteen to twenty miles. Coaches every three or four hundred. Drivers often. Brush wickiups! For people to sleep in! Or on the ground! Who watches the mail bags? An Indian could steal them. That's no way to run a stage company."

"It's a wide country and mighty empty," St. John said.

"I know. So we've got to put in enough men. How many did the Birch Line have? How many horses?"

"Something over sixty men," St. John said. "They use mules. About four hundred."

"No wonder they can't run a stage line!" John Butterfield snorted. "We'll have two thousand horses. As many men. Only a hundred or so stations to start, but we'll have more than twice that. Now tell me. Our engineers have crossed once. New country to them. You've been out west five years. Made three round trips over the Birch Line. What's this empty country like? How are the roads? And how about these deserts and no water?"

"If you're from New York, you wouldn't call them roads," St. John said. "From San Antone to El Paso, where you won't go, freighters have left a good set of wheel tracks and the Army's fixed up some of the bad spots. El Paso west, the Army's been working, but not always on the route you'll take. After Yuma you hit a real desert, the Colorado. The Birch people don't even try to run stages across. Take passengers and mail on mule-back for a hundred miles. Sand's too deep, though I understand a good trail can be made in Mexico until you're half way across California."

"Yes," Butterfield said. "My men found that. But these deserts. Isn't there any water?"

"In spots, and they'll make your trail look like

Bands of Indians would attack and run off the mules

a rail fence. Only way to cross is to go from water
hole to water hole. Or dig wells. Some emigrants
and the Army tried that. Got water in a few places.
But there are others where you can't. Just dry
desert. Never a drop across the Gila Bend. They

call that the Forty Mile Desert. Then from the
Concho to Horsehead Crossing on the Pecos in
West Texas—I haven't been over that but I've
talked with men who have. Seventy miles with no
chance of water. The Army even tried drilling

out there. Had to go down a thousand feet to find it."

"My engineers have told me. I've already ordered special tank wagons built. I'll build tanks at the stations, haul water to them. Because we've got to have something for men and horses to drink. How hot do these deserts get?"

"You can fry eggs on the rocks," St. John said. "We didn't have thermometers but I've heard it gets to one hundred and twenty in some places and higher than that at Yuma and in the Colorado Desert in California. The Birch people sometimes travel at night and lay up in the daytime to save the horses. I hope, Mr. Butterfield, that I haven't discouraged you. I thought you wanted the facts."

"And nothing else," John Butterfield said. "And I'm not discouraged."

Next day he talked again with Silas St. John, on the subject that bothered him most—Indians.

"The Birch people have any trouble with them?" he asked.

"Quite a bit," St. John said. "Nothing big, like a mass attack. But small bands would tackle us in camp. Mostly to run off the mules. Maybe, if they saw a chance, to attack us. We didn't have much they wanted except firearms and ammunition. They'd burn the coach and mail, take clothes and what little grub there was. Indians don't take big risks. They're too smart. They maneuver to get all the odds. But they have taken a lot of mules and killed a few people."

"We'll go armed," John Butterfield said. "Every man will have a rifle and revolver. But why doesn't the Army stop them?"

"Your worst stretch is Yuma to Fort Chadbourne in Texas, about eleven hundred miles. The Army has four or five forts on your route. If it had twenty, the Indians could still slip through and around and do as they please. They're smarter and better desert fighters than the Army, and from all I've seen and heard, I don't blame the Indians for hating the whites. They've had plenty of cause."

John Butterfield wasn't interested in that. He thought only of getting the mail through, and he

The Indians watched the troops go through Apache Pass

had been told many times an Indian was not to be trusted.

"I'll put extra men clear across that thousand miles," he said. "Well armed. It'll take a lot of Indians to whip them if we have stone stations and corrals, good protection."

"Your stages have to run between stations, and there are plenty of places for an ambush," St. John said. "But you have two big chunks of luck, Mr. Butterfield, though no telling how long either will last. First, down in West Texas. Comanches have kept Texans out of there since the first white men appeared. They raided straight across your route, clear to East Texas at one time. They would have stopped you dead a year ago. They're bad. They hate white men and never miss a chance to fight."

"What's happened to them?"

"The Texas Rangers and a band of Tonkawa scouts gave them a sound beating last fall. Really put the fear in them. But there are a lot of fighting Comanches, and they may break loose again."

"How about the Apaches?" Butterfield asked. "I hear they're really bad."

"That's your second piece of luck. Two years

ago Major Enoch Stein marched to Tucson to take over the Gadsden Purchase and built Fort Buchanan near the Mexican border. That was in the territory of the Chiricahua Apaches, a small band but well organized and trained as warriors. Their headquarters are smack above Apache Pass, which you'll have to go through because there's no water to the north or south. It's narrow, rocky. The Chiricahuas could stop you dead."

"Why doesn't the Army drive them out? How can the government expect me to take mail through if I have no protection?"

"It isn't necessary. Every white man out there hates an Apache, but from all I could learn, the Chiricahuas' chief, Cochise, is quite a leader. He saw Kearny's and Cooke's troops go through and decided he couldn't lick them. So when Major Stein arrived he got in touch with him, arranged

67

a meeting, and made peace. Cochise guaranteed that any white man going through the pass or his territory would not be harmed."

"You can't trust the beggars," John Butterfield said.

"Cochise has kept his word for two years. Not a white man has been harmed. You'll have trouble along the Gila with the Tonto Apaches, and across New Mexico and West Texas with the Mimbres Apaches. But in the Chiricahuas' land you'll be safe—unless some fool white man starts something."

The more John Butterfield talked with the young fellow, the more he liked him and understood how valuable an employee he could be. He reached a decision.

6

NEXT DAY WHEN ST. JOHN ENTERED THE OFFICE, John Butterfield said, "This is Bill Buckley, son of Henry Buckley, who was driving stage out of Albany when I was born. Bill is as good a driver as I had in the Mohawk. He's been roaming through Ohio and Kentucky, picking up the best drivers for us. And horses. Now he's going to be superintendent of our Sixth Division, from El Paso to Tucson."

Buckley shook hands. He was a big man, gruff and aggressive, and clearly he wasn't impressed by the frail young chap before him.

"Tomorrow Buckley is leaving to establish a line of stations between Fort Smith and Tucson," Butterfield said. "It will be a rush job. The first stage starts September sixteenth, and it's got to go through. The stations must be operating, with crews, horses and spare stages, stocked with feed. St. John is going with you, Bill, and when you get down in Texas, he will select the station sites."

Buckley didn't like that and showed it.

"Bill," John Butterfield said, "you never saw a desert, a real mountain or a wild Indian. You never knew thirst or desert heat. You've driven stages only on fair to good roads. St. John crossed to California by ox team. He's been in the West five years. He rode on the first Birch stage out of San Diego. He's made the round trip, San Antonio to San Diego, three times on the Birch Line. He knows the roads, where to get water, where the Indians are, where we should have our stations.

He knows things none of us know, and I'm trusting him to do a good job. You're boss, but St. John is to pick station sites and best routes."

Early in the spring of 1858, Silas St. John and Bill Buckley started west from Fort Smith, on the edge of what was then civilized America. One step and they were in the Indian Territory, now Oklahoma, and 200 miles beyond was West Texas, big, empty and scarcely known.

They had a long train of freight wagons heavily loaded with supplies and many men, and more trains would follow. After Fort Smith they had little trouble. Choctaw Indians had been living there more than thirty years, had farms and fair roads. Several of these Indians became "home-station" keepers and helped keep the roads in repair—one operated a ferry by which stages crossed into Texas.

This was heavily wooded country, and many

Silas St. John and Bill Buckley started west with a long

settlers had established farms and cut roads. Counties were organized and helped build the post route. But beyond Jacksboro the country opened into wide flat or rolling plains. This was Comanche country, and the settlers did not dare go farther. A dozen years later the Comanches and Kiowas were still raiding.

train of freight wagons heavily loaded with men and supplies

Buckley failed to find anything startling in North Texas. "I've seen the same thing in parts of Ohio," he said. On the plains he found no signs of humans except a string of four Army posts leading into the southwest. Stations had been built at each. Beyond was nothing, and Buckley's contempt for the country began to lessen. Here was desolation such as he had never imagined. When they made the seventy-mile traverse from the Middle Concho to the Pecos, with no water except what they carried in barrels in the wagons, he was troubled.

"We ought to have two stations across there," he said. "Maybe three or four. And we'll have to haul water to them."

"You haven't seen anything yet," St. John said. "And if we're going to have stations where we really need 'em, across New Mexico and Arizona, we haven't time to stop now. Only way to get across this place is to relay mule teams, driving them in a herd along with the stages."

They reached the Pecos River and followed it to the New Mexico line, crossed and turned west. Before the crossing Buckley saw Guadalupe Peak seventy miles west.

"We'll make it by night," he said.

St. John smiled. "You'll get used to that from now on," he said. "We'll need at least one station between here and that mountain."

"You're crazy! Look at it, man!"

"Ox team freighters have told me they've watched the peak for a week and never seemed to get any closer."

When they'd spent nearly three days reaching the Guadalupes, Buckley began to mutter to himself. "Something's wrong," he said.

They came to El Paso, after establishing twenty stations beyond the North Texas settlements. They'd dropped off wagons and men but still had a long train. Each time a wagon went back, they sent a report to John Butterfield. Now, through the worst of the Apache country, they needed more supplies. Butterfield had sent supplies on, but not enough men, so they hired Mexicans along the Rio Grande.

John Butterfield had sent messages too, arriving weeks afterward, of course. They urged, urged, urged. They kept repeating, "The stages must start September 16. We must have stations, relays of horses, everything ready."

"He's a driver," Bill Buckley said. "Of horses and men. That's why he's a stage man. But this sort of country—it just ain't natural. I don't think John can do it."

"He'll do it," St. John said. "You can't think anything else after talking to him. And as for the country, and Indians, you haven't seen anything yet. But we've got to get busy. It's three hundred and sixty miles to Tucson, where we should meet the California people. Not a white man, not a fort, after we leave the Rio Grande. We ought to have twenty stations. We'll be lucky to get a dozen built."

Building stations was far more difficult after leaving the settled and wooded North Texas. Little timber could be found, often none. It was simple to throw up a log building and fence a corral, something else to split stone and erect high walls for a corral and houses of stone and adobe. Also, John Butterfield had ordered all stations in Indian country built like forts, of stone or thick adobe, so his men could defend themselves and could not be burned out.

"If the stages get through, it will be because John shoved from behind with his own arms," Buckley said. "And maybe he will at that. Let's start."

They went up the Rio Grande with a long wagon train, established a station at Fort Filmore, last Army post they would see in more than 300 miles, went on to Mesilla and crossed the river, climbed to the high mesa and followed the Birch Line most of the way. They did not build as many stations as were needed.

"No time now," St. John said. "They can come later."

They left a wagon and crew at Cooke's Springs. The route wandered too much, Buckley thought.

"Water," St. John said. "We'll even zig-zag later. From spring to spring. No hauling water in this country. No spring, no station."

They swept up the long grade toward the continental divide in New Mexico. To north, south and west, mountains showed above the skyline, and never got nearer.

"Take us a month to reach 'em," Buckley muttered.

The train was kept together, and if a wagon broke down or fell behind for any reason, the others waited. Every man except the Mexicans carried rifle and revolver at all times. Scouts on horseback ranged ahead and on the sides. Each night the wagons were drawn in a circle and several guards were placed.

"We're getting into the worst Apache country," St. John said. "Mimbres Apache country. Mangas Colorados is their chief. Plays hot and cold, hot if he thinks he has a chance. They're the tribe's biggest band. Range back into Texas. But the old boy doesn't like to tackle a train like this. He'd lose too many men."

"How about the stations?" Buckley asked.

"We've got to leave more men. Scare 'em so they'll keep constant watch. After they get up stone walls, they'll be fairly safe."

They crossed New Mexico without incident. St. John knew Apaches watched every step, but they did not see an Indian. Wagon after wagon was dropped with its crew, and the crews worked fast to build walls. No man ever went into the southwest without having proper respect for Apaches.

The train entered Arizona, plodded across the San Simon Valley and reached Apache Pass.

"Now we needn't worry," St. John said. "The stronghold of Cochise is on top of those mountains. He hasn't touched a white man for two years, and many settlers have gone past. I drove through the pass six times and never saw an arrow. Saw Cochise once at the spring. Fine looking fellow, tall, and proud. If he were against us, no stage would go through."

They left a wagon to build a station at the pass. Time was getting short, and the wide Arizona desert stretched before them.

"We'll have to skip stations here, build them later," St. John said. "Next water is Dragoon

They hauled flat slabs of rock for the ten-foot wall

Springs, at the north end of the Dragoons, forty miles. The Birch Line crossed it in a day."

"We should do it in six hours on this level going," Buckley said. "But no water—it will wreck the horses."

"Then we'll have to wreck them. It is eighty-two miles from Dragoon Springs to Tucson and we have time to build only one more station, that at San Pedro River. In less than four weeks the stages will start, and Butterfield wants nothing less than stone forts through here, he's so set on keeping off the Indians."

"What you figure then?"

"I'll stay with a wagon and men at Dragoon Springs. You go on to the San Pedro and build there. That's only twenty-three miles, but twenty-four miles beyond are the Cienega Springs, where teams can be watered. Then it's only thirty-five miles more to Tucson, where our job ends."

"You've been over this route six times and ought to know," Buckley said. "Me—this is no country for man or beast."

At Dragoon Springs, beneath the western stronghold of the Chiricahua Apaches and now not occupied, Silas St. John stopped with a wagon-load of supplies while Buckley went on. The trail was plain, having been used by the Birch Line.

With St. John were five Americans and three Mexicans, the last hired in El Paso. To the Americans, who had never seen real desert country, it was a forbidding land. In certain lights the Dragoon Mountains above them looked as if they were solid steel, with bare sides and sharp crests. To the west swept the great San Pedro Valley, unbelievably wide. Morning and night the colors changed, distances grew or lessened. Always there was an impression of emptiness, of lack of life.

The men began work at once. They hauled flat slabs of rock in the wagon and erected a ten-foot wall around an enclosure 55 feet long and 45 feet wide with only one opening, a gate through

83

which a stage could be driven. The gate would be heavily barred with timbers. Inside, in two adjoining corners, they built rooms of rock, each about ten feet square, but not yet roofed. The job went swiftly, the men working long hours under St. John's urging. He was greatly impressed by the planning and energy of John Butterfield, was now a warm admirer of the stage man, and he wanted to see the stages roll on time.

The morning of September 7 he sent two Americans west on horseback to help Buckley at the San Pedro. Remaining with him were James Laing of Kentucky, James Burr from Watertown, N. Y., who was to be a station blacksmith, and Preston Cunningham of Iowa, a man really too old for western hardship but who had stood up remarkably well. Also he had the three Mexicans, and St. John trusted them to the point where he had them stand their guard watches at night.

All worked hard September 8, cooked supper and turned in. The heat was oppressive and the men were exhausted. St. John slept in one corner room, Cunningham in the other, Laing in a shed and Burr outside the gate with the Mexicans. Laing stood the first watch. At midnight, St. John roused a Mexican to relieve Laing. In the bright desert starlight he saw all the others sleeping soundly and went back to bed. Before dawn he was wakened by a whistle, shouts and groans. As he sat up the three Mexicans appeared in the door, swinging two axes and a sledge.

7

SILAS ST. JOHN COULD SEE DISTINCTLY, THE ROOM having no roof. When the first ax descended he rolled away, but not soon enough. It caught his left arm, nearly cutting it off above the elbow.

He rolled back, and another ax slashed his right forearm. Other blows cut his hand and inflicted a deep gash in a hip.

Back and forth he rolled, trying to dodge blows and reach his weapons. In the small room, the Mexicans were slashing wildly. He got his Sharp's rifle, but his left arm was useless and the weapon was too heavy to be fired with his wounded right.

When he picked up the rifle, the Mexicans backed to the door and gave him a chance to get his revolver. He fired and they fled. Evidently they did not know how badly they had wounded him, for they did not come back. But St. John expected them. He could not understand why they didn't come. Outside he could hear the groans of the others. They were as helpless as he.

Pain and loss of blood did not permit him to get up. He kept the revolver ready, but when the attack was not resumed he managed, with his badly wounded right arm, to twist a tourniquet on his left. The bleeding became less, but not until daylight did he have strength to crawl out of the little room.

In the other room he found Cunningham. The old man had been slashed three times through the skull with an ax but was still alive. He did not know St. John had come. Under the shed was Laing, also unconscious but terribly wounded. Just outside the gate lay Burr. He was more for-

He fired, and the Mexicans fled into the desert

tunate. His head was crushed by the sledge. He was dead.

St. John could not do anything for them. He was too weak. Each movement sent blood gushing from his wounds. The desert sun beat into the corral and unroofed buildings. He had nothing to drink, and the spring was too far for him to hope to reach it. He lay on a pile of grain sacks, getting what shade he could from the wall. His clothes were stiff with caked blood. He ripped his shirt apart and bandaged his wounds with one mangled hand.

Mules were tied inside the corral, in the hot sun. They brayed for water, stomped and tried to break loose. Night came. Cunningham died. Laing still moaned. The attack had come after midnight Wednesday. Friday morning vultures and crows came and sat on the wall. St. John waved at them, but they returned and at last began tearing at the body of Burr, pecking out his eyes and ripping flesh from his face, neck and hands.

Friday night wolves came. St. John fired his revolver at them, but they kept coming back and tearing at Burr's body. All Saturday he wondered how much longer he could last, how soon the wolves and buzzards would be tearing him apart. Pain and weakness brought semi-delirium. Sunday morning he could no longer fire his revolver.

As he lay waiting for death, he thought often of John Butterfield, of the tremendous task the man was attempting, and of how one little slip, such as his own at Dragoon Springs, could ruin a great enterprise. The first stages, one from the East and the other from the West, would start in a few days. They would count on finding water and a relay at Dragoon Springs, on a team harnessed and ready, and beyond was the long dry run to Tucson with only the one stop Buckley was building.

St. John blamed himself for trusting the Mexicans and giving them guard duty. He felt he should have known better. He understood how the three had planned it. After the two Americans were sent on to the San Pedro, the Mexicans could kill the four remaining Americans in their sleep, take the mules and wagons, all the supplies, and go to Mexico. It wasn't far, with good going up the San Pedro. They'd be rich for a year.

The injured man got some satisfaction. The Chiricahua chief, Cochise, had kept his word not to harm Americans, but he had refused to cease fighting Mexicans. They had been Apache enemies for three centuries. St. John knew Chiricahua scouts were always roaming their domain. They'd be sure to see the fleeing slayers. Probably the vultures were already picking at them.

Sunday morning St. John was surprised to discover he was still alive. His tongue was so swollen from thirst it stuck out of his mouth. He knew another day of desert heat, wounds and lack of water would finish him. While he lay there, hoping to die quickly and be rid of his agony, a white man bent over him.

He was an Army man, of a road-building crew bound westward. Water was brought and St. John and Laing were cared for as best the party could. A messenger was sent at once to Fort Buchanan in the Sonoita. What was left of Cunningham and Burr was buried. The mules were fed and watered. Next day Laing died.

Friday, nine days after St. John was wounded, an Army surgeon arrived and immediately amputated his arm at the shoulder. On September 23, eight days after the first Butterfield stages had departed, he was taken to Fort Buchanan in an ambulance. The man's vitality was remarkable. Thirty days after he was attacked he mounted a horse and rode to Tucson, forty-five miles from the fort.

The three Mexicans were never seen again in the United States. They may have escaped, but St. John was confident that the vigilance of Cochise and his Chiricahua Apaches had brought vengeance.

8

JOHN BUTTERFIELD, BACK IN ST. LOUIS, HAD never ceased to drive. He kept freight, men, horses, stagecoaches, tank wagons and equipment moving in a constant stream to the southwest. It irritated him that he had to wait so long to know what was happening in that great void. Weeks and even months passed before he could learn how many stations had been built, what additional supplies were needed, how well his men had repaired the worst places in the road.

In the Mohawk Valley his own telegraph company could bring reports. Here he had to depend on the slow tread of freight trains or a messenger traveling a thousand miles on horseback. Always, he felt, he was working in a vacuum. He'd send stuff out and not know what happened to it.

In midsummer he felt he had to have something definite on which he could base his hopes, so he arranged test runs from Tipton, end of the 160-mile railroad headed westward, to Fort Smith and on into Oklahoma. Some runs were encouraging, others not. His drivers from the Mohawk said they had never seen worse roads.

"We wouldn't drive a farm wagon over some of those stretches back in New York State," one said. "And people lived there. What's it like where nobody lives, all the way to Californy?"

John Butterfield refused to be discouraged. He felt he couldn't be. He had to win. The mail had to go through. And he knew his Mohawk men.

They'd grouch and complain but, once on the driver's seat with reins in their hands, they'd not let anything stop them. They'd always recall:

"Remember, boys! Nothing on God's earth must stop the United States mail!"

He was even more uncertain about what was going on in the far west. He had sent trusted men from New York, and they had hired drivers and others who knew California stage roads and conditions. The Butterfield engineers had refused to accept one route demanded by the Postmaster General, through San Gorgonino Pass and south in the Salton Sink to the Mexican border. No water was to be found the entire way and summer heat in the sink "would melt the iron tires off the coaches." A new route had been found through rough mountains and still across the desert but with some water. John Butterfield tried to imagine a land without water.

Indians worried him too, the Comanches and Apaches. He wrote often to Washington, demanding forts and protection, but nothing happened, so he bought more rifles and revolvers and planned to have ten men at some of his most vulnerable stations. He sent more tank wagons out to haul water when he got reports from St. John and Buckley.

Usual details of a stage route, adapted to an empty country, were taken care of. By September first, all stations were manned, so far as John Butterfield knew. Horses and coaches were sent out to stations as far as Tucson, and east from San Francisco. Grain, hay and other supplies had been distributed. Veterinarians were patrolling their sections and looking after the animals. Blacksmiths, harness makers and wheelwrights were placed at intervals to keep horses shod and repair vehicles and gear.

Expenses mounted. Two thousand men were drawing wages. Hay cost $43 a ton in California, could not be bought over half the route and had to be freighted in. Each station required up to 100 tons a year, unless there was good grazing near by. Barley was $5 a bushel, freighted to Fort Chadbourne in Texas, only the beginning of an empty 1,000-mile stretch. And always 2,000 employees and passengers must be supplied with food, though no food was to be had within a thousand miles.

September 16, 1858, approached, with John Butterfield still driving ceaselessly, attending to last minute details. The night of the fifteenth he sat in his St. Louis office with Young John. He could do no more. At eight o'clock next morning the first mail sacks would leave on a train to Tipton. Yet he could not relax. His job would not be completed until the first east and westbound stages had completed 2,800 miles and had arrived on time. He could not loosen the tension.

"One year!" he said. "For a job like this! They've been talking of a railroad across the country since 'Forty-five, and in thirteen years they've got only as far as Tipton, a third of the way. Field started his Atlantic cable more'n a year ago after years of getting ready. He got a message through to Queen Victoria and then the thing broke. No telling when he'll get it working. It took 'em eight years to dig the Erie Canal. But this stage line! Long as the cable and across a country as empty as the Atlantic! With a twenty-five-day limit! We got to be running in one year, and not a day over."

Young John knew his father was letting off steam and only trying to relax. He'd worried about the older man's strain. It had never lessened. Now his father smiled suddenly.

"Know who's going to drive the first west-bound stage?" he asked. "Start it right? It isn't just hoping for a lucky token that I'm picking you. You're like I was. Not happy unless you've got four reins in your hands. Tomorrow you'll have 'em."

Young John grinned. He'd been working hard,

Mail and passengers were transferred to the stagecoach

helping his father, and he'd been hoping for this chance.

"So get to bed," John Butterfield said. "Train leaves for Tipton at eight in the morning—*of September sixteenth!*"

which was waiting when the train pulled into Tipton

That day started badly. St. Louis and its newspapers had forgotten the Butterfield Line and gave it no heed. Six passengers had been booked, five as far as Fort Smith and only one through to San Francisco. Two small leather mail bags held less than fifteen letters. More than a million dollars and a year of effort and anxiety for this!

But John Butterfield held his head high when he accepted the pouches and rode to the railroad station in a wagon. The train departed at eight o'clock, a funny little affair of a few freight cars, baggage car and a little passenger coach, all drawn by a tiny locomotive with a wide flaring stack. It couldn't quite make the 160 miles in ten hours.

At Tipton a new, brightly painted stagecoach was waiting with six of the company's finest horses stomping and pretending to be frightened of the train but easily held in place by handlers at each bridle. Only a few of the hamlet's people were on hand to watch the beginning of a great adventure, but John Butterfield was no more disturbed than a year earlier when he had been accused of planning only to sell stock and clear out.

He was still a stagecoach man. In the few minutes required to transfer mail, passengers and baggage to the coach, he walked along both sides of the team, examining harness, adjusting a buckle. Satisfied, he waved to his son and the conductor on the driver's seat, and entered the coach. They were off, to the music of the conductor's horn and the clatter of hoofs as the horses broke into a gallop. They were off—into the bright light of a sun setting in the unknown west, off to success or failure.

Young John kept the horses at a gallop all the way to the next station, seven miles. The station keeper had a big fire burning beside the road in celebration, and his wife set a hot meal on the

The road got really rough as the stagecoach

table. Only twenty minutes were permitted for
eating, and with a fresh team they were off. All
night they rolled, the horses galloping where they
could, the coach lurching and rattling and the

entered the Ozark Mountains in the night

passengers bouncing about. Sleep was next to impossible. Stops were made only to change teams.
Dawn came and passengers saw the campfires
of emigrant trains and people stirring about. They

saw fields and cattle and farm houses, for this part of Missouri had been settled thirty years earlier. All day they rushed on, changing teams. Greatest distance between stations was twenty miles, often half that. In mid-afternoon of the second day the coach arrived at Springfield, where John Butterfield and Young John received the first recognition of their achievement. A crowd had gathered to cheer them, and to watch them switch from a Concord coach to a "celerity wagon." It took three-quarters of an hour.

Now the road got really rough as it entered the Ozark Mountains in the night. The coach rattled over rocky roads and swung around turns above cliffs. Long after dark, Young John was relieved after more than twenty-four hours on the driver's seat. The road became worse. "The stage reels from side to side like a storm-tossed bark and the din of the heavily ironed wheels in constant contact with the flinty rock is truly appalling," one traveler wrote.

At two o'clock the morning of September 19 the first westbound stage reached Fort Smith, a town of 2,500 but really the end of civilization and the last community until El Paso was reached. It had covered 318 miles since seven o'clock the evening of September 16. Though long after midnight, the citizens turned out and held a celebration. Metropolitan St. Louis might not notice the start of the new mail route but out in the wilds, where communication meant so much, the people cheered John Butterfield. To them, he was a hero. Now they could get letters from the East in less than ten days.

The stage on the Memphis branch arrived a few minutes before that of the main line. Despite the celebration, a quick change to new coach and team was made and in minutes the coach rattled on into the southwest. John Butterfield left the stage here. The other passengers, stiff, sleepy and bruised, had reached their destination. Only one went on over the entire route.

He was Waterman Lily Ormsby, 23 years old, a reporter on *The New York Herald*. His paper believed in the new mail line and had sent him west to ride the first stage. If he had known what he was in for, he would never have left New York. But he stuck it out. Without him we would have had no story of that first 2,800-mile trip of the Butterfield Mail because stage drivers don't write. Ormsby sent back dispatches each time he met an eastbound stage and they were published, often weeks later, in *The New York Herald*.

9

Young ormsby was a good sport. in the beginning he was inclined to compare the comfort of the stages with that of horse-drawn cars on Fifth Avenue, and the food with what he had eaten in New York. He had never been west, knew nothing of an empty, primitive land, but he was curious and eager and soon became excited over the adventure. Physically he took a beating. He had two meals a day, and their spacing was uncertain. He rattled and banged around the empty coach, and only complete exhaustion brought sleep. This continued for nearly twenty-four days.

He had company to Fort Smith—John Butterfield and the other passengers. The road was rough, and the drivers were pressing the horses. Each felt he had to get through on contract time, and some of them took chances. But the country was understandable, with farms, villages and towns. It was not too unlike the East. In Oklahoma there were tidy farms and small settlements with quiet, industrious inhabitants. Ormsby was surprised to learn they were Choctaws, members of the Five Civilized Nations who had been transplanted from eastern states. On one brief stop Ormsby gave an Indian boy "a paper of tobacco" to get water with which to wash his face.

Along the northern fringe of Texas he found white settlers, mostly from Virginia, Kentucky and East Texas. They had not gone far west because of the Comanche Indians, who later drove them out. Here he found a change, first in meals. At an early morning stop the men at the station had overslept, or had no faith the stage would arrive on time. They had no plates or forks, only four cups for six people, who waited in line for coffee and ate the only available food—corn cakes baked in the ashes.

Ormsby was getting into the real West, and drivers were not wasting a minute. He'd paid an Indian boy for water to wash his face, but when he reached the Clear Fork of Brazos River he saw a chance to get a bath. In a brief stop he took soap and towel and dashed to the stream. The driver wasn't waiting, the conductor tooted his horn, and Ormsby hurried back, drying and dressing himself in the coach as it hurtled on into the southwest.

It was the southwest now, as he quickly learned.

The timber was behind him. The country rolled and spread endlessly. Farms and settlements no longer slipped behind. Coaches raced through a land in which nothing seemed to live. This was no longer a stage on a New England or New York post road. This was raw and dangerous. Some stations were still being built and men slept in tents, cooked meals over open fires. Stoves were unknown. Even in a completed station the cook worked at an open fireplace. And here were Indians wholly unlike the Choctaws.

The first stage reached one station to discover that Comanches had attacked it and run off all the horses, leaving only a few unbroken mules. The stage had to go on if it were to make contract time, and Butterfield men were determined it would. Mexican herders gleefully roped, threw and harnessed four mules, and dragged them to their places in front of the coach.

Two hours were spent in the task. Ormsby, watching the operation, decided the coach would be wrecked and he would be badly injured or killed in the middle of nowhere. He said he would wait for the next stage rather than risk his neck. J. B. Nichols, who had driven for Butterfield in New York, did not seem to be concerned.

"These mules want to run," he said. "We'll let 'em. Make up for the delay."

"But they'll wreck us," Ormsby said.

"I don't think so. They'll calm down after ten miles."

Nichols knew how important it was to have the reporter go through on the first stage, and he argued. His own confidence was the deciding factor. When he went to the driver's seat, Ormsby climbed up beside him. The Mexicans, sitting on the heads of the mules, looked up, grinning. This was going to be fun.

It was, though not for Ormsby. At Nichols' signal, the Mexicans jumped away and the released mules scrambled to their feet. Each tried to take off in a different direction but the harness, traces and Nichols' firm hands on the reins held them to the road. They were frightened and mad, wanted only to rid themselves of harness and the lumbering thing behind them. So they had nothing to do except run.

Ormsby had sat beside Nichols because he thought he had a chance to jump if the coach was tipped over. He hung onto the seat rail, terrified. They had left as night came, and he could scarcely see the dim road ahead. Nichols was watchful but calm.

"How far is the next station?" Ormsby asked.

"I believe it is thirty miles," Nichols said.

"Do you know the road?"

"No. I have never been over it."

"Then how do you expect to get there?" the reporter demanded.

"There is only one road, and if there's only one, how can you miss it?"

"Indians raided the station last night. They might try to stop us. Are you armed?"

"No," Nichols said. "And I don't want any guns. Besides there's no danger."

The Mohawk Valley man from New York, who had driven only over safe roads in a settled country, was unperturbed. Firmly he guided the wild mules along what was not a road as he had known it but only a pair of wagon tracks across a wide, desolate stretch of prairie land that could not grow a tree or a bush.

Ormsby settled down. The moon came up, full, and lighted the way ahead. He began to enjoy the wild scenery and the sense that he and Nichols were alone in a world of their own, a strange world

When the westbound stage passed the eastbound

stage, every man fired his weapons in celebration

for a New Yorker. Later he spelled Nichols ﺎ
the reins and had a new thrill. He felt he was
somewhere between the Atlantic and the Pacific
and that it didn't matter much where. Nichols
slept beside him, and he slept while Nichols drove.

Next morning they reached a station and got
a fresh team and new driver, a meal, and went on
into the worst stretch of the entire route, from
the Head of Concho to Horsehead Crossing on
the Pecos River, seventy-five miles without a drop
of water. Canteens were filled and, as there had
not been time to build stations and tanks and provide relays of teams, a herd of wild mules was
driven ahead of the stage to provide changes.
Later several stations and water tanks were built
on this route, but when Ormsby crossed they had
to do the best they could.

But "nothing must stop the United States mail,"

and nothing did. The stage made the crossing and, without pause except for change of teams, swept up the east side of Pecos River, turned west toward the Guadalupes. They cleared the pass, in which it had been necessary to blast out rocks to permit passage of the stages. Ormsby lost all command of his language here. This was the real West and all he could say was that "the wild grandeur of the scene is beyond description."

Meanwhile another stage was traveling this route. It had left San Francisco September 14. Now, after striking east from El Paso into Apache country, it was using an "outrider," who went ahead and on the sides as an Apache camp had been reported. In a draw he fired his rifle and yelled "Halt!" Eastbound passengers piled out, weapons ready, expecting an Indian attack. One was a representative of the Postmaster General, known today only as "G. Bailey" (the name signed on his report), who was making the first eastbound trip.

Indians did not attack. It was only the first westbound stage. The two passed, everyone firing his weapons in celebration. Each was ahead of schedule. Many bets had been made as to where the first stages would pass, El Paso being the favorite choice. They met about 100 miles east of that town.

The new driver who took over at Horsehead Crossing was Capt. Henry Skillman, who had worked for the Jim Birch Line. He drove all the way to El Paso, 306 miles, with only seven changes of horses, a tremendous feat of endurance.

From El Paso the road followed the Rio Grande to Mesilla, then turned across the New Mexico uplands rimmed by distant mountain peaks. Apaches ranged far into Texas but this was their

Cochise looked down from the canyon sides

country. The Mimbres of Mangas Coloradas had headquarters just north of the route. As the coach raced westward the chief and 250 of his warriors were holding up a Butterfield supply train at Stein's Peak station in Arizona.

"Want twelve sacks corn quick," the Indian said.

He got it, at once. The freighters, knowing the first stage was due, did not want trouble. When the stage arrived, after racing across the high, hard plains at what Ormsby estimated as an average of nine miles an hour, the Apaches merely watched it. Mangas Coloradas told a station man he believed the government had an interest in the line and soldiers would come if he molested it.

Ormsby, the sole passenger, was whirled on into the West. Next station, thirty-five miles beyond, was the once dreaded Apache Pass. A chief sat on his horse and looked down from the canyon side. Behind him were ranged a few warriors, none in war paint.

"That was Cochise," the station agent said when they stopped to change horses. "We don't worry about him."

They stopped at Dragoon Springs, where Silas St. John had been so seriously wounded less than three weeks earlier, and Ormsby got the details of the fight with the Mexicans. He wrote the story at length, the first with gory overtones he had found in the southwest. This he sent to *The New York Herald* by the next stage he met. Otherwise St. John's experiences might never have been known.

The stage went on to Tucson, the ancient town of adobe walls and houses, north to the Gila River and across the Forty Mile desert. Beyond was Oatman Flat, where Apaches had wiped out an emigrant family seven years earlier. Now they were in a real desert, and nearing sea level with heat intense even in October. They were ferried across the Colorado into the Sand Hills country, not unlike the Sahara, and were forced south into Mexico.

Famished for water, they neared a vital well north of what is now Calexico on the California border. Here, for the first time after 2,000 miles, Ormsby was faced with real Indian trouble. A band had decided to stop this and all future stages and just outside the station they blocked the road. The stage stopped and driver and conductor picked up their rifles. The crew of the station swarmed out with their weapons and opened fire. The Indians had only bows and arrows and a few muzzle loaders. They retreated soon. The stage got a fresh team and sped on.

Los Angeles, then a town of 6,000, largely Mexican, was included in the route only because

Butterfield's engineers had refused to go through the Salton Sink. Now the town had no interest in the mail stage when it arrived in early afternoon. Los Angeles had stage connections with San Francisco on a road along the coast, but the Butterfield Line ran north through Tejon Pass into San Juaquin Valley, and over this 462-mile stretch the route led northwest.

Ormsby was now back in civilized country. Settlers had been coming for ten years or more, many from the East. When Butterfield's stagecoach reached Visalia, the town put on a celebration, the first since Fort Smith in Arkansas. These people wanted to hear from the East, and they found the stage mail far ahead of that which came by steamship via Panama.

North they sped, on better roads and at a far faster pace than anywhere on the route. In Pacheco Pass, Ormsby was really scared for the first time. On downhill grades "Tate" Kinyon, the driver, refused to use the brakes but only cracked his whip. His passenger estimated their speed at fifteen and even twenty miles an hour.

"We flew at a rate which I know would have made old John Butterfield, the President of the Mail Company, and a very experienced stage man, wish himself safely at home," Ormsby reported.

After Pacheco Pass the stage had a level road all the way to San Francisco, and the young reporter needed it. He had been riding now for more than twenty-three days and nights. Never had the stage stopped except for meals and to change horses. The roads had been rough and often dangerous, and the lone passenger had no chance to sleep in a bed, rarely to wash his face. He wrote that, after a few days, exhaustion compelled sleep no matter how he was battered about the lunging stage. He must have had bruises and black and blue spots over most of his body.

But he was exalted as the coach dashed into San Francisco at sunrise the morning of October 10, 1858, the horses galloping through deserted streets. It was not only that he was the first man to cross the continent in less than fifty days. He thought of John Butterfield, back in St. Louis, and wished he could tell him the route had been traversed in 23 days, 23½ hours—more than a day under the contract time. No one believed it could be done. Now it had been.

In St. Louis the departure of the first stagecoach had not aroused interest. Now San Francisco was unaware that the St. Louis coach had arrived. Perhaps the city did not believe anything so spectacular could be accomplished. It gave no heed to the first eastbound stage, or to the six that followed, two each week. But excitement grew when the city woke up later that Sunday morning

When people in San Francisco realized what had hap

and understood that mail and newspapers had come from the east days faster than the best steamships and weeks ahead of the intermittent service through Salt Lake City. This was what they had been asking of Washington for years.

The town turned out. The newspapers got busy

pened, they turned out to celebrate the first overland mail

a day or two late. On Monday night a salute of thirty-two guns was fired in Portsmouth Square, opposite the Butterfield station and a celebration was staged in the Music Hall. Ormsby was the chief speaker, and his description of the trip aroused both interest and laughter.

The San Francisco Bulletin and *The Daily Alta California* immediately arranged to start reporters over the route and send back dispatches. When the second coach from the East arrived October 15, streets were crowded, bands played and salutes were fired. Letters poured into the post office. Passengers applied for seats until there were not enough stages to carry them. No one had believed such speed over 2,800 miles was possible. Now it had been proved.

10

JOHN BUTTERFIELD DID NOT KNOW HE WAS A hero in California. For more than three weeks he had been pacing his office in St. Louis. In the last year, minutes had been more precious than dollars, and he had poured in the dollars. He kept sending men and supplies into the southwest after the first stage had gone, though he had no means of knowing whether he had failed or won. He could telegraph to New York and get a reply. San Francisco might as well have been on the moon.

On October 9 the first stage reached Tipton

from San Francisco. Mail and passengers boarded the train for St. Louis. John Butterfield had gone ahead to Jefferson City and boarded the train there. Twenty-four days, eighteen hours and twenty-six minutes after leaving the Golden Gate, mail and passengers were in St. Louis. The telegraph flashed the news from Jefferson City; and St. Louis, which had ignored the Butterfield Line, turned out to welcome the man from Mohawk Valley with bands, a parade, and speeches. John Butterfield was pleased, but this wasn't to his liking. He was distressed by the oratory and more distressed when he was asked to respond. He spoke briefly but was glad to get away from the crowd at the end.

"I'd rather drive a stage across the Sahara Desert," he said to Young John afterward.

Still he did not know what the first westbound stage had done. Eastbound stages reported passing it but definite news of its arrival in San Francisco could not come until the first week in November, nearly two months after its departure. As John Butterfield waited, he received two messages from Washington. President Buchanan wired, "It is a glorious triumph for civilization and the Union." And Postmaster General Brown wrote, "I rejoice in your success."

John Butterfield went to Tipton, hopefully, a day or two early. If that first stage reached San Francisco within the contract time of twenty-five days, he had won.

The eastbound stage came, a bit ahead of time, the horses galloping all-out down the main street of the village and plowing to a stop before the station.

"Hey, John!" the driver shouted when he saw his employer. "Yip-eee! Twenty-three days and twenty-three hours! Yip-eee! Yip-eee!"

The reinsman from the Mohawk had become a westerner, and no Texan ever put more feeling into that original cowboy yell.

John Butterfield grinned broadly, but the news did not bring relaxation. Suddenly, for him, the job had just started.

"We'll cut that to twenty-one days!" he said to Young John. "We'll run six stages each way weekly. Forty-five or fifty on the road every minute of the day and night."

"That's a lot o' stages," his son said. "And across twenty-eight hundred miles."

"No one believed we could run one in twenty-five days. Even those California stage men wouldn't believe it. Washington didn't. They thought I was stock-jobbing. Now I'll show 'em something."

John Butterfield hadn't waited for this moment before improving his stage line. He had already sent men and supplies into the southwest to build more stations. He'd not had time in that first year, though with the home stations and those already established in much of California, he had provided 150. He'd known, to get speed, he must have 100 more, especially in that vast empty and dry land between Fort Chadbourne in Texas and Los Angeles. He'd like to have a station every fifteen miles. Then, with quick changes, he might cover the route in twenty days.

"We'll show these westerners," he said, not thinking that few white men had been born in the West, that nearly all had come from the East and South, that the gold rush had started only ten years earlier.

As John Butterfield crowded men and supplies onto the long road, other troubles came. The first were successes, and demanded quick attention. The route as far as Fort Smith was so popular it was necessary to put on more coaches and run a daily passenger service. Then gold was discovered in the desert east of Yuma, and prospectors flocked in. More passenger coaches from Los Angeles were needed to race the treasure hunters to the new field. A year later, the demand for transcontinental transportation was so great that bookings were made weeks in advance and premiums of $100 were paid for seats.

Indians became a menace. They rarely molested the station agent and his crew, but they did steal horses in large numbers. The Butterfield Line had better steeds than the prairie mustangs, and every Comanche and Apache wanted one. Thefts became so great that often stages arrived at a station to find no relay. Every head had been run off, and weary horses had to go on to the next stop.

Someone told John Butterfield that Indians considered it beneath their dignity to be seen riding a mule, so from the Texas line on to California he withdrew what horses were left and replaced them with mules. What he did not know was that Indians liked mule meat better than most any other. The raids continued, and the drain on the company was heavy.

Indians wouldn't ride a mule, but they loved mule meat

The government also caused trouble. It cut out the center of the Birch Line, from El Paso to California, and turned it over to Butterfield. Later it added the El Paso-Santa Fe route to his lines, which now totaled more than 3,500 miles.

All this meant more men, more and more horses and mules, more feed to be freighted into the desert, and more wagons and stagecoaches. In the beginning, John Butterfield had doubted the ability of the famous Concord stagecoach to remain upright on the rough roads of the far West. He designed a lower coach, with smaller wheels, but longer. Upper weight was cut by using a canvas top and sides. The interior was arranged with wooden seats, not upholstered, the backs folding down to form a platform, or bed. Such a coach was unknown in the East, where taverns provided sleeping places, but Butterfield foresaw the night-and-day drive across the country and provided some means of sleeping. He called these "celerity wagons."

The Concord stage was the elaborate affair so well known on eastern post roads, with high wheels and an enclosed wooden body. Some were painted red, others green, and the undercarriage yellow. Sides and doors were decorated, some with original paintings. Across the top was "Overland Mail Company." The interior was padded and curtained with leather. Construction was heavy throughout to withstand speed on rough roads. At the rear was a boot that would hold 600 pounds of mail, and in some models a seat was built above it for the conductor.

Nine persons could sit inside, swaying and bumping. As more mail was carried, until it was greater than that in steamships from New York to San Francisco, sacks were stowed under seats, further crowding the passengers. And they had to take 2,800 miles of that, without rest! The coaches cost $1,400 to $1,500 each, and now John Butterfield needed more.

Fares were established at $200 westbound and $100 eastbound, and no one has ever understood why the difference. It was soon changed to $150 each way. Way fare, between any two stations, was ten cents a mile. Meals, twice a day, were extra and cost forty cents to a dollar. Early travelers found a great difference between the food in Missouri, Arkansas and California and that in the long central stretch where milk, eggs and vegetables were unknown. Dried beef, venison, bread baked in ashes of open fires, coffee straight and bitter—men had to live as best they could, and no one objected too much.

On the earlier Birch Line it was more difficult. A California paper recommended that each passenger carry a Sharp's rifle, Colt's Navy revolver and 150 rounds of ammunition. Also changes of clothing, blankets, socks, underwear, needles, hair brush, soap, and plenty of food that did not require much or any cooking. But Birch Line stages stopped each night to camp, with passengers sleeping on the ground and preparing their own meals over an open fire.

Except to Fort Smith from St. Louis, and San Francisco to Yuma, no reference has been found to women riding on the Butterfield Line. It was too rough. It is doubtful if they could have stood it, and in that first primitive year at least they could not have had privacy. In crowded celerity stages, passengers had to take turns sleeping, and those who slept had to wedge themselves against others or be thrown across the stage.

John Butterfield knew this, and he planned to build a series of taverns in which passengers could stop over, get a night's sleep in a bed and catch a following stage. This would give a man a chance to shave, bathe and rest. William Tallack, an Englishman on his way home from Australia in 1860, wrote of the lack of bathing facilities. He said some passengers, even in the heat of the summer desert, did not bathe or change underclothing on the entire route, and rarely washed their faces.

Crossing the continent on the Butterfield Line also became something of a sporting proposition. Passengers and stage crew always carried weapons, and no one knew when an Indian attack might come. Two young men, eastbound from San Francisco, had a particularly fine day. Their names are not known, but their story was picked up by later travelers and verified by Butterfield Line employees.

Their adventure started with a desire for a bath after the long dusty journey in California. Often the stages halted at a station on the Gila River so passengers could wash off the desert grime, but

this stage was behind time and the conductor refused to wait.

"All right," the young men said. "We need a
bath. We'll hire saddle horses and overtake you."

"Fool thing to do," the conductor said. "Tonto
Apaches all along this stretch. They haven't the
guts to tackle a loaded stage, but they'd like nothing better than pick off two men traveling alone."

"We'll chance it. Got to have a bath."

They rolled in the warm water, scrubbing off
the dust, dried quickly in the desert air, and
mounted their horses. Each had a rifle and revolver and plenty of ammunition. The horses were
fresh. Miles ahead the dust spiral rose from the
stagecoach.

"Indians didn't stop it," one said.

"These stage men see an Indian behind every
bush," the other said.

Apaches had been watching the stage, hoping
something would happen to it. They didn't ex-

Two passengers stopped at the Gila River for a bath, but

pect two mounted men to follow, and when they saw fine horses, rifles and revolvers, they went into action. The young stage passengers found themselves attacked on both sides and in front.

the stagecoach driver was behind schedule and drove on

"Go through!" one yelled. "Our only chance!"

They raced ahead, shooting fast. Only two Indians had old muzzle loaders, the rest bows and arrows, and Apaches were too smart to take short risks. Those ahead gave way and then, first from one side and then the other, they charged close, one at a time, hoping an arrow would strike home. They hung low on their horses, leaving only a swift, small target.

The white men slowed down so they could shoot better. One hit a horse, and its rider struck and rolled, did not get up. A bullet knocked an Indian from his seat, and the horse went on alone. The Indians became more cautious but more angry. They played the game with true Apache skill, riding along the sides of the road, darting in and out.

For miles it was a running battle, a dozen against two. The white men answered war cries with derisive hoots, and shot as straight as they could.

They killed a second Indian and a third. That was enough for the Apaches, who rarely took the short end of a bet. The two passengers went on and caught the stage. They felt they'd had a grand time.

Those Tonto Apaches established one record. Though many attacks were made across 1,500 miles of travel, they were the only ones to destroy a station, Gila Ranch at the bend of the Gila River. Also, in nearby Pima Pass, they ambushed a stage and killed a company official. Far to the east in Texas, Comanches became bolder and attacked stations, sometimes decorating the log walls with arrows and once setting fire to a building and forcing the crew into the open. Usually the station men were too well armed and protected to permit a successful onslaught, but the Indians continued to run off horses and mules as they wished.

One station keeper in Arizona tried to outwit

The white men slowed down so they could shoot better.

the Apaches by teaching his mules that, when he
beat on an iron gong, it was feeding time. They'd
come in at a trot. If he heard Indians in a raid at
night, he'd sound the signal. Sometimes it worked.

In the skirmish one Indian was knocked from his horse

One legend has come down from those days that was pure legend. This is of mounted Indians riding beside a stage and filling it and its passengers with arrows while conductor and passengers knocked the braves off their steeds with rifles and revolvers. It just never happened, despite the thousands of paintings of such scenes and the countless movies.

The Indian, and especially the Apache, was a clever and calculating warrior. Always he wanted all the odds he could get, and he couldn't get them when riding within ten feet of a rifle. When he did attack a stage it was in a narrow canyon, with himself behind a rock and with all the advantage of complete surprise. The legend of running battles grew out of Buffalo Bill Cody's Wild West Show of sixty years ago, and it was a good act. His famous Deadwood stage raced around the arena surrounded by Indians, and hundreds of rounds of blank cartridges were fired. It was thrilling and exciting, and artists and movie people have believed it ever since.

11

JOHN BUTTERFIELD, IN ST. LOUIS, NEVER SAW HIS great line of stagecoaches thundering across the west. He never went past Fort Smith, but he knew everything that was happening, knew all about each station and what every mile of road was like. Also, he was probably the first land transportation man in America who recognized the value of minutes and seconds. The clipper ship masters racing around the Horn to California and China had also understood the importance of speed. Before the first stage started, a timetable was prepared, and drivers were expected to keep it. No allowance was made for the many ferries, meal stops and team changes. Stages, he said, were expected to travel faster than schedule to make up for such delays.

An old stage driver himself, John Butterfield knew how to point up his instructions. He showed that if each driver lost fifteen minutes, the total loss would be more than a day on the entire route. His reinsmen, who were from New York and Ohio and strange to the west, understood. And never while John Butterfield operated the line was the contract limit exceeded. These drivers fell in too with his suggestion that a gain of ten or fifteen minutes would give leeway for accidents or other delays. He had drivers who knew what he meant, and they scared many a passenger as they forced teams over rough roads. They even killed or injured passengers with upsets in the Ozarks.

Instructions to employees had a military touch.

Each was expected to give all his time to the company, whether he be station herdsman or driver. Always mail was to be guarded. He didn't write it, but his men knew the old order: "Remember, boys! Nothing on God's earth must stop the United States mail!" And they let nothing stop it.

John Butterfield was never satisfied with success. He wanted more stations to insure faster time and aimed at a twenty-day schedule. He wanted more comfort for his passengers and planned taverns across the land. He said once he expected to have his coaches traveling 30,000 miles each day, an unheard-of achievement, and he might have done it. Certainly his stages made one trip from St. Louis to San Francisco in nineteen days.

He had all the plans made and much of the work done for the greatest stagecoach line in history when suddenly his health failed. The strength which had carried him since he'd watched the Albany stages pass his father's farm was gone. He had never rested, never taken a vacation. For three years he had devoted every moment to accomplishing what men said could never be done.

His illness was serious and in April, 1860, he returned to his home in Utica and for two years was an invalid. He was in his sixtieth year, considered old at that time.

Under the impetus he had given, the Butterfield Line continued its record-breaking service. The stages went through on time. Horses were changed on an average of fifteen miles. Grain and hay were grown in the rich Mesilla district on the Rio Grande, and in the Santa Cruz valley near Tucson. There, after he had lost his arm at Dragoon Springs, Silas St. John was appointed agent for the Gadsden Purchase and put in charge of the Papago, Pima and Maricopa tribes, all peaceful and agriculturalists for centuries. He arranged for Butterfield to furnish seed, and the Indians grew much grain for the stage line.

St. John returned to New York in 1860 and was an executive in an express company until 1896, when he retired and went west. He died in San Diego in 1919, 84 years old.

The stages went through but, in a way, the service became worse. Ormsby, on the first westbound trip, wrote that he did not find an employee who was not courteous and helpful. Two years later the Englishman, Tallack, made some of them out as a vile lot, and old employees agreed with him. Many of the Mohawk men followed their leader back to New York. They could not imagine driving a stage without John Butterfield owning it. Their places were taken by men from Ohio and Kentucky.

Other forces, over which John Butterfield himself could have had no control, were building up. These forces were far above stagecoaching, above spanning the continent. First were the Apaches, who always had the power to stop the line, unless each coach were accompanied by a company of cavalry. Second was the growing feeling in the South that it must break away from the Union, even if that meant starting civil war. Against either one, the Butterfield Line was helpless. Perhaps it is lucky, for John Butterfield, that he was far away when the trouble started, that he knew little or nothing about it.

Except for stealing horses and mules, the Apaches had caused little trouble. The Tontos, along the Gila, were the worst, but they didn't stop the stages. In West Texas, Apaches later stopped all traffic, though Army posts were scattered along the line. The Mimbres, under Mangas Coloradas, in New Mexico, were the largest band, but their chief was cautious and 500 heavily armed miners in the Santa Rita district, close to the stage line, kept them from aggressive action. After John Butterfield retired, a small band ambushed a Santa Fe stage on the Rio Grande and killed driver and conductor.

The Apaches who could have stopped the stages any time they wished gave no trouble whatever. They were the Chiricahuas, whose chief, Cochise, had given his word to Major Stein that white men would always be safe when crossing his territory. He never broke that word, given in 1856. Mules, horses and crew were safe on the eastern Arizona desert. A renegade Chiricahua, Geronimo, who operated from Mexico, often raided New Mexico stations for mules and horses.

John Butterfield had given strict orders about Indians. No intercourse was to be had with them, and they were not to be annoyed or incited to attack. Always a strong guard was to be maintained. Most employees were from the East and more or less afraid of the Indians' reputation and were glad to obey the rules. Exceptions were in the Chiricahuas' country where Cochise had guaranteed safety. The chief often went to the Apache Pass station beneath his stronghold in the Chiricahua Mountains, or to the Dragoon Springs station above which his west stronghold towered. He cut wood and traded it for supplies at Apache Pass, brought in a few gold nuggets and was always friendly. The station people learned Spanish and a bit of Apache and soon had great respect for the Indian as a man of honor. He liked to watch the stages pass.

Ten months after failing health forced John Butterfield's retirement, the great tragedy of the southwest began at the Apache Pass station. A rancher in the Sonoita appealed to the commander at Fort Buchanan to recover his stepson, half Mexican and half Tonto Apache, who, he said, had been captured by the Chiricahua Apaches and was being held in the east stronghold of Cochise. The Army man did not believe it. Cochise had kept his word for more than four years and had caused no trouble of any sort. The rancher returned again and again, demanding action and recovery of the boy, known as Mickey Free.

At last the commander gave in. A second lieutenant, George N. Bascom, fresh out of West Point and just arrived in Arizona, was sent to investigate and bring back the boy. He had a detail of twelve men, all experienced Indian fighters and with a sergeant who knew Cochise and believed in the Apache's word. Bascom thought he knew all about Indians, though he had never seen one up close.

He led the detail to Apache Pass and made

camp a mile from the Butterfield station. At the station were the agent, C. W. Culver, a hostler named Welch and a driver, J. F. Wallace, laying over for his next trip. All had been there a long while, knew Cochise well, and admired him. Bascom left word with them that he wished Cochise to come to his camp.

Cochise, through his scouts and smoke signals, knew all about Bascom's detail and wondered what it meant. He had kept his word with the Army and, after four years, trusted the Army to keep its word. When he received Bascom's message, he was curious but not disturbed. He went to Bascom's camp with his wife, a young son, two nephews scarcely adults, and his brother, of whom he was very fond. Perhaps he became suspicious when he saw a flag of truce flying over Bascom's tent, and he took a quick and appraising look at the shavetail. A supreme military commander himself, Cochise understood the false dignity of a young officer.

Cochise and his people were invited into the tent, and immediately a guard was thrown around it. Bascom was waiting inside, and he had no smile of welcome. He had read much about Indians, felt sure he knew all about them, that they were not to be trusted and must be dealt with sternly. His own men had tried to tell him Cochise was a man of honor and could not have stolen Mickey Free, and the Butterfield station men had backed that up with their own opinions of the Apache chief's integrity. They even pointed out that they had only three men in Apache Pass while other stations in Indian country had eight or ten.

Bascom was not impressed. He was of the Army and not taking the opinions of civilians or enlisted men. He would handle this in his own way, the Army way.

Not understanding that a conference with Indians must proceed slowly, with a long pause before negotiations begin, Bascom began at once with a demand that Mickey Free be returned to his family. He was not impressed by the astonished statement by Cochise that he knew nothing of the boy. Abruptly, Bascom called the chief a liar, and he repeated the words.

Nothing could have insulted Cochise more. He was proud of his word, of always keeping it, and jumped to his feet with a howl of rage. With a slash of his knife he slit the tent and leaped through and ran past the guard. The soldiers fired and a bullet hit the Apache's leg. But he ran on, weaving and dodging until he escaped. His family tried to follow. A nephew received a severe bayonet wound. The others were captured.

Cochise ran to his stronghold and gathered the few warriors there, raced to the stage station. The

Butterfield men knew nothing of what had happened and came out readily when he called. Culver and Welch, unarmed and trusting the man they knew so well, approached the chief. Apaches surrounded them. They fought clear with their fists and ran to the station. Both were shot and killed.

Cochise had wanted them as hostages to exchange for his relatives. When Bascom's troops appeared at the station, he withdrew. Apache scouts reported a freight train approaching and Cochise sent men to capture all Americans. They got two, and eight Mexicans. The last were tied to the wheels and the train set afire. The Americans, names unknown, were taken to Cochise.

He had another and bigger scheme to gather hostages and, knowing the westbound stage was due, had dried hay placed on the road, to be set afire and stop it. The stage was two hours early, reached the station before dark and went on. Its passengers saw the roasting bodies of the Mexicans as they passed. They must surely have warned those on the eastbound stage. However, Buckley the driver, determined to go on.

Next day Cochise appeared above the station with 100 warriors, all in war paint, and they awed even Lieutenant Bascom, who had only a dozen men to back him. The Apache leader offered an exchange of prisoners. Wallace, who liked Cochise and trusted him, thought he could end the trouble and went out to talk it over. He was captured, and Bascom refused to consider an exchange of prisoners.

Meanwhile, the eastbound stage was due, and Cochise had placed warriors to stop it and capture more hostages. Bill Buckley, superintendent, was riding beside the driver. The passengers were all alerted and ready with their revolvers when the

Apaches opened fire. A mule was killed, and the driver was shot in the leg. Passengers jumped out, firing at the canyon walls. They cut the dead mule loose and Bill Buckley, son of the Henry Buckley who had saluted John Butterfield and his mother more than fifty years earlier, lashed the team on to the station. At the gate another mule, wounded, dropped dead. All got behind the stone walls of the corral.

Next day Cochise appeared with his warriors and another offer to exchange prisoners. Bascom's sergeant and the stage people urged him to accept.

"Those are white men," they said. "He'll torture them to death if you don't."

Bascom, the shavetail, was all Army, or thought he was. He refused to consider the matter until Mickey Free was returned, and at once, before his eyes, a mounted Apache warrior dragged Wallace to death along the mountain side. Cochise went

When the warriors of Cochise opened fire on the stage

coach, the passengers jumped out, firing at the canyon walls

to his camp and tortured the two unknown Americans until they died. An Army detail arrived from Fort Buchanan with three more prisoners, picked up on the way, and they, with the brother and two nephews of Cochise, were hanged. The wife and son of Cochise were taken to Fort Buchanan where they were released. They made their way home, a hundred miles across the desert.

Bascom, arrogant and ignorant, had set loose a tornado which swept all white men from southern Arizona. Within a year he was killed in a battle with the Confederates on the Rio Grande. He died without knowing he had lighted the fuse to the bloodiest Indian war the United States has had. He knew only that the Army had praised him for his action at Apache Pass.

For a dozen years Cochise held the Army helpless. Generals who had fought through the Civil War admitted he was their superior as a military man. His warriors were far better trained, his smoke signals far faster and more efficient than Army communications. Apaches killed or drove out every settler, miner and rancher in southern Arizona except Pete Kitchen at Nogales. No white man was safe outside the walls of Tucson and Tubac. Never has the United States Army suffered greater humiliation. And Cochise never had more than 600 warriors.

The second force, which also would have overwhelmed even John Butterfield, ended his stage line. The Bascom tragedy in February, 1861, came when the Butterfield Line had been operating with such astonishing success for two and a half years. Less than a month later, Congress decided to move the route to the north, in safer territory. South Carolina had seceded from the Union in December, 1860. The Confederate States of America were formed a few days before

Bascom so grievously insulted Cochise at Apache Pass. In April, 1861, the Civil War began. Before then, Texans had been holding up stages and running off horses and mules. And the North had to have communication with California and its gold.

Cochise did not start his war at once. He was wounded, he had to consolidate other Apache bands in a confederacy to drive out all Americans, and when he was ready in April, just as the Civil War started, the Butterfield Line suddenly disappeared.

Physically, the change to the route through Nebraska, Wyoming, Utah and Nevada was smooth. Stages at each end simply were started on the new line. Those on the way completed their three-weeks' trips and began again on the overland route to the north. The last coaches through were stopped in Texas but, because they carried United

States mail, they were allowed to go on. When the war started in April, the last had escaped.

If the war had not come, Apaches still would have been able to stop the Butterfield Line. From the Rio Grande to Los Angeles, water was imperative at each station, and Cochise and his men needed only to capture strategic springs. What Cochise planned was to capture the stations with their arms, ammunition, grain and other supplies.

He and Mangas Coloradas got a few. The long freight trains moved slowly, were vulnerable. Oxen and mules meant food and rifles were to be had. Many Apaches had only bows and arrows and needed weapons, powder and ball. The Indians had a free hand. Before war started, all troops were ordered east. The desert country was left without protection and settlers and miners were slaughtered by the hundred.

Despite the Apache uprising and withdrawal of

soldiers, officials of the line kept at work for several months, closing out stations and examining claims for damages of those who operated "home stations." All completed their work and escaped to the north, except seven young men employed in the El Paso office.

These seven, one only nineteen, provided the final example of loyalty to John Butterfield and his stage line, and to the Union. They worked as clerks, drivers and conductors in El Paso, center of the route and most important station between St. Louis and San Francisco. All were from the north. The El Paso station was the most ambitious John Butterfield had built, a large adobe building of Mexican style, and in it they were trapped when civil war broke out.

They had much work to do, guarding the extensive property of the company and cleaning up details of removal to the north. While they knew the Civil War had started, they felt they must remain until the work was completed. Communications were slow or non-existent, but they did know Texans were with the South and soldiers of the Confederacy were moving west, with California in view.

They knew they could not get out to the east through Texas, the Indian Territories and Arkansas. The South would bar the way. Perhaps they could have gone north to Santa Fe and beyond, but they decided to go west. They'd find safety in California and a way back home. They didn't think, or know, of the Apache uprising, or of summer heat in the desert.

Plans were kept secret, a "celerity coach" was loaded with company records and not enough ammunition and food. Before dawn of a July morning they eluded southern sympathizers and started north up the Rio Grande. No one stopped them. They reached Mesilla, crossed the river, headed west and felt safe. Before them was the high reaching land of New Mexico, rolling and rising to the continental divide.

They stopped at company stations each night, at Picacho, Rough and Ready, Goodsight. They saw no one, and a smoke signal far ahead meant nothing to them. One evening they reached Cooke's Springs, a station selected by Silas St. John in 1858. It was small, with a tiny room in a corner of the stone corral. They watered the mules at the spring a quarter of a mile away and brought back water for themselves. While they were cooking supper the Mimbres Apaches attacked.

It was not serious. The Indians' scouts had kept careful watch and knew how many men and horses were in the party, but they could not understand why these white men were going west, why a stage was covering a route that had been abandoned for four months. So the first onslaught was only exploratory.

The seven white men, caught off base and a bit frightened when they saw so many Indians circling the station, fired from the top of the stone wall, and as darkness came they saw the Apaches disappear. Two dead or wounded were carried away.

"We taught them a lesson," said John Wilson.

"Maybe not," said Emmett Mills, youngest of the party. "They'll be back, most likely after dark. We've got to stand guard, and we ought to have more water."

Four went out to get the water before dusk, and to give the mules a final drink. It was the final drink. The Apaches attacked at dawn, their favorite time. They came by the score, riding to the walls of the corral and shooting at the men inside. An arrow went through Champion's heart.

Robert Alvin was wounded but kept firing. That day they killed nine Apaches.

The second day was worse. Alvin died. Freeman Thomas and Joe Porcher were killed. John Pontel was badly wounded and died that night. Only the youngest, Emmett Mills, and John Wilson were left, and Wilson had been pinked by an arrow. They killed ten Apaches, could count the bodies lying outside the corral, but this brought no hope.

"They'll get us tomorrow," Emmett Mills said. "I only hope we get a few first."

Two of their mules had been killed, and the others were dying of thirst in the desert heat. Mills and Wilson rationed what little water was left. Their ammunition was getting low.

"Maybe we should have gone up to Santa Fe and tried to get through that way," Wilson said.

"Or get home by way of the moon," Mills said.

Bodies of the five dead lay where they had

fallen. There had been no time or strength to care for them, and digging graves in the sun-baked soil would have been difficult. Before dark, Emmett Mills wrote a note, explaining what had happened and giving the names of the five who had been killed and the two who survived. He placed it under a stone pulled off the wall. He and Wilson cooked supper, and didn't talk much. Through the night they stood alternate watches.

The Apaches came back at dawn. They had spent twenty men to kill five, and that was not the Apache way. But the Indians were riding a wave of excitement and anger. They were incensed by what had happened to Cochise at the hands of Lieutenant Bascom and inflamed by the withdrawal of the Army. This land had always been theirs, and they intended that no white man was to live in it.

Mills and Wilson, their ammunition low, held

their fire until they felt they could surely kill. For hours the Apaches swept up in waves. An arrow killed Wilson. Mills counted the twenty-third dead Indian, and then a bullet hit him in the head. Later, when no fire came from the station, the Apaches swept in. They stripped clothes from the dead and mutilated the bodies with knives and axes, took what loot they could find and departed.

Two days later a freight train, one of the last to brave Apache vengeance, passed Cooke's Springs. Buzzards, a black cloud of them, told what had happened. The leader went inside the station. He found the bodies and buried them. He found the note Emmett Mills had written and took it with him. If he had not, details of the battle would never have been known.

This was the final chapter in the story of the Butterfield Line. Perhaps John Butterfield never heard of it as he was still seriously ill in Utica.

But he would have liked that story. He would have known his men were still faithful. Those seven young chaps who made the Indians pay three to one were not carrying the United States mail, but they were living up to the Butterfield tradition.

Meanwhile the stages were running on the shorter mid-continent route from St. Joseph, Missouri, to Placerville, California. The Butterfield Line lost much equipment and money in making the transfer. Indian attacks were far more frequent in the north. The first winter's snows slowed and even stopped traffic. Stages were to run six days a week. Mail piled up in the delays and some was lost or destroyed. The Overland Mail Company got into financial difficulties. Ownership and contracts changed hands.

It simply was not the old Butterfield Line, with John Butterfield holding the reins and snapping the whip. He had made a success over a new route which no one had believed possible. He had kept schedules better than the railroads and against far greater odds. Perhaps it was as well that he collapsed when he did. Either the Apaches or the Civil War would have beaten him on the southern route. War and political maneuvers would have beaten him on the central line to California.

In 1869 John Butterfield died of a stroke, probably his second or third. It is doubtful if he was aware of what had happened to his dream, or that no other man came near matching his success in spanning an unknown continent.

Strangely, the "Overland Mail," which never approached his performance, received all the credit in fiction, the movies and history and became impressed in the popular mind as the single and only transcontinental route. Yet Butterfield preceded the central route and set a mark it never matched. He preceded the Pony Express, the telegraph and the railroad and carried untold tons of mail and uncounted passengers on the swiftest journey horses have ever provided.

Only where he operated does John Butterfield's memory remain. In the southwest the words "Overland Mail" are rarely if ever heard. It is "The Butterfield Line." State maps show its course. Railroads and main highways use its route or run close to it. Scores of towns and cities straddle the marks left by its iron wheels. Highway markers erected by states, local organizations and women's clubs point pridefully to the fact that the greatest of all coaches and four passed at certain points.

After nearly a century the signs of his roaring stages remain. They cut deeply into wet adobe mud and have been baked by desert sun. The heavy tires scored sandstone and lava and granite, and the marks are still to be seen. Heaps of stone and adobe tell the sites of his stations, where horses were changed so swiftly the driver had only time to light his pipe. Find an old timer in dozens of small towns and he will proudly point out the course of "The Butterfield Line."

Perhaps the greatest tribute to John Butterfield was that of his son, Daniel Adams Butterfield, who emerged from the Civil War as a major general. While in service he composed the music of "Taps," familiar to millions of United States soldiers. He must have had his father in mind and played it first on a coaching horn.

Index

LANDMARK BOOKS

★